CEPHALONIA
& ITHAKI

EDITIONS
TOUBI'S®
ΕΚΔΟΣΕΙΣ

ATHENS 2001

© Copyright 2001   MICHAEL TOUBIS PUBLICATIONS S.A.
                    Nisiza Karela, Koropi, Attiki.
                    Telephone: +30 210 6029974, Fax: +30 210 6646856
                    Web Site: http://www.toubis.gr

ISBN: 960-540-065-0

On the window where you lean
no carnation is befitting.
You are the carnation
and whoever has eyes
can see it.

Traditional arieta

CONTENTS

CEPHALONIA

1. INTRODUCTION

2. HISTORY

3. CULTURE
AND TRADITION

CONTENTS

4. A TOUR OF CEPHALONIA

ITHAKI

~1~ CEPHALONIA

Cephalonia is the largest of the Ionian Islands, and its name may be related to this fact, as one possible meaning may be that of the 'head'('kefali') of the Ionian Islands. According to another old version, the island was the homeland of the mythical hero and king Cephalus or the homeland of the ancient people known as the Cephallinians or Cephallanians.

Cephalonia is a land of contrasts. Peaceful beaches and bays are succeeded by coastlines that cut abruptly into the sea. Elsewhere, the forests, covered in the singular Cephalonian fir tree, generously proffer their shade, creating a unique variation in landscapes. Here, the suspense of the sea meets the mystery of the caves, which hide their treasures well. During the festivals of the Panayia (Our Lady), the whole of the natural environment is transformed in honour of Her.

Cephalonia:
an invitation to fairy-tale writers.

a journey without end

This is only the beginning.
The island certainly has more surprises in store.
Goats with golden teeth, who quench their thirst by inhaling (!) the damp
breeze, sea water which does not heed the conventional laws of nature,
spilling out in great rifts close to the shore, creating the so-called
Katavothres. Abandoned castles, dragon caves and caves where nymphs
reside are yet more of the wonders of the island.
Cephalonia sticks to its fairytales. It sticks to their teachings, to the
awe that they inspire in the common folk, in their heroes.

Not that it won't please the lovers of the good life as well.
How could it be otherwise?
The island's tourist facilitates are of excellent standards and able to
satisfy the highest demands, whilst the hospitality of the residents
is exactly that expected of an island where Xenios Zeus
-Zeus the Hospitable- was once worshipped.
Yet, Cephalonia provides you with another opportunity.
The opportunity to go on a dream journey to magic worlds, to
distant eras. A journey which excites the romantic
and arouses the dreamers.

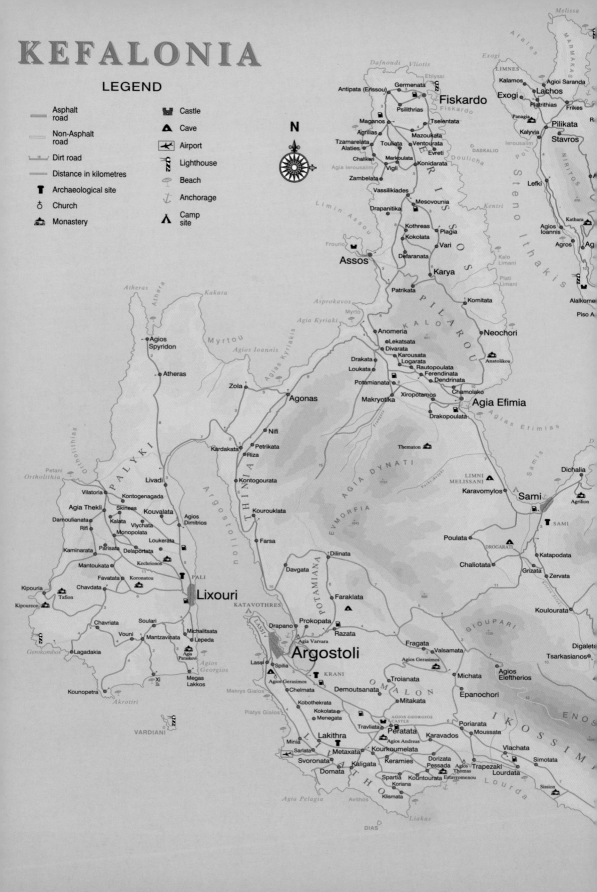

Geography

Position: Cephalonia is the largest of the Ionian Islands, with a total area of 688 square kilometres. It lies to the south of Lefkada and Ithaki and to the north of Zakynthos, opposite the mouth of the Gulf of Corinth (or Gulf of Patras).

Morphology: The island is mountainous (more so than any other of the Ionian Islands), with peaks running from the most northerly cape (Dafnoudi) to the extreme south (Cape Mounta). Mt Ainos, in the south, is the highest of the mountains, with its tallest peak, Megalos Soros, reaching up to 1,626 metres. Mt Ainos, popularly called 'Megalo Vouno' (the big mountain), is covered by a very rare species of fir tree (Abies cephalonensis). Among other mountains are Ayia Dinati (1,131 m.), Roudi (1,125 m.), Kokkini Rachi (1,082 m.), Xerakias (1,068 m.), Omorfia (1,043 m.), Sella (1,000m.), Merovigli (993 m.), Vrochonas (946 m.), Avgo (929 m.), and Kalon Oros (901 m.). The island's few small plains are in the districts of Kranaia, Omala, Sami, Pylaros, Livadi and Pali. A large amount of pluvial water is retained in the Omala and Pyrgi areas, where the large lake Avythos, or Akoli, at Ayios Nikolaos has been formed. The coast is indented, and there are numerous bays and capes. The most important bays are those of Sami, Myrto, Argostoli, Lourdas and Livadi, while the capes are as follows: Vathi, from south to east, Mounta, Kapros, Sarakiniko, Mytikas, Kentri; Dafnoudi is in the north; Atheras is to the north west; Ortholithia, Skiza and Yerogombos are to the west and Akrotiri and Ayia Pelagia to the south once more, followed by Liakas, Kastanas, and so on. On the mainland side, the coastline tends to be relatively easy to approach, while on the Ionian Sea side cliffs rise above the sea shore. The island's caves are of especial interest, such as the precipices of Melissani, Angalaki, Ayii Theodori, Zervatis, the Drogarati cave, the Sakkos cave. etc.

Climate: The climate of Cephalonia is generally mild, with typical Mediterranean island features, that is a dry summer and a wet or mild winter.

Local administration: the local administration of Cephalonia is divided in the following way: the Municipality of Erisos, the capital of which is Vasilikiades, the Municipality of Pylarion (capital Ayia Evfimia), the Municipality of Argostoli (capital Argostoli), the Municipality of Pali (capital Lixouri), the Municipality of Sami (capital Sami), the Municipality of Livathos (capital Keramies), the Municipality of Eleios -Pronoi (capital Pastra). The capital of the township of Omala is Valsamata, whilst there is a separate Municipality of Ithaki, the capital of which is Vathy.

Prevailing winds: North-west 23.3%, north 14.8%, south-west 14.3%, south 11.8%, north-east 9.3 %.
Strongest winds: NE and E (not stronger than gale force 5). Seasonal features: winter, north-easterly winds; summer, north-westerly winds.
Frequency of windless days: 13.5%.
Temperatures: Annual average, 18.5⁰ C, highest monthly average 22.3⁰ C lowest monthly average 13.8⁰ C highest recorded 40.2⁰ C (August) lowest recorded, -2.2⁰ C (February).
Rainfall: Annual average: 1084.7 mm.
Distribution: winter: 525.2 mm (48.5%);
spring: 173.7 mm (15.5%)
summer: 26.6 mm (3.0%)
autumn: 359.2 mm (3.30%).
Annual days of rain: 107.7 (45 in winter, 5 - 6 in summer).

Geology

The geology of the island of Cephalonia is characterised by the unification of two geotectonic zones. The western section, which is also the largest, is part of the Paxis zone, whilst the eastern section is part of the Ionian zone.

The Ionian zone is limited to the south-eastern section of Cephalonia. It is composed of sedimentary rocks which were entirely formed beneath the sea that lay between the underwater mound of the Paxos zone to the west and the mound of the Gavrovo-Tripolis zone to the east. In this marine area, which existed for several million years, rocks of an almost uniform type were formed, i.e. mostly limestones. Only during one short period, from the Middle to the Upper Jurassic period (180 million years ago) did sections of this marine area dry up. We can divide the sedimentary rocks of the Ionian zone into three general groups:

In the lowest section, which dates from the Triassic to the Jurassic periods, that is 245 to 170 million years ago, shallow marine rocks were formed (limestones, dolomites, and evaporites). The next group was formed at a deeper level beneath the sea, consisting of sedimentary rocks from the Jurassic to the Upper Eocene (170 - 35 million years ago). There follows a third group to which belong sedimentary rocks that indicate that the region was beginning to rise, i.e sedimentary rocks of a much younger age with flysch characteristics (which indicate emergence from the sea). This emergence was completed during the Aquitanian-Burdigalian stage (the past 21 million years).

Within the rocks of the middle group, that is during the submergence of the sea, there was plenty of life, with many organisms of the cephalopod class of molluscs, which are now found as ammonoids, fossilised in the sedimentary rocks of Cephalonia. These cephalopods no longer exist and became extinct over 65 million years ago, along with the Dinosaurs.

The Paxos Zone, to the west of the island, which constitutes the greater part of Cephalonia,

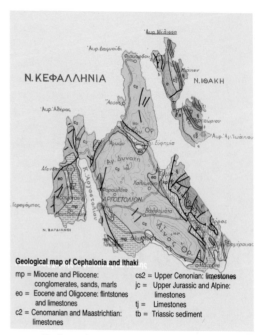

Geological map of Cephalonia and Ithaki

mp = Miocene and Pliocene: conglomerates, sands, marls
eo = Eocene and Oligocene: flintstones and limestones
c2 = Cenomanian and Maastrichtian: limestones
cs2 = Upper Cenonian: limestones
jc = Upper Jurassic and Alpine: limestones
tj = Limestones
tb = Triassic sediment

Geological map of Cephalonia and Ithaki.

is made up of a continuous series of carbon sedimentary rock in a shallow marine area. This section was located beneath the sea (although not at a great depth) from the Upper Triassic period until the Oligocene period (235 to 25 million years ago). It emerged later than the Ionian Zone.

The sedimentary rocks that make up the western section of the island include evaporites, dolomites and shallow marine limestones. This layer is around 1,500 metres thick. During the Upper Cretaceous period (97-74 million years ago) the sea was dominated by flat-gilled aquatic crustaceans (shells), the fossils of which we can find in abundance in Cephalonia today. To the west of the islands of the Ionian Sea is the Hellenic margin, along the length of which is the great movement of the Hellenic arc.

This movement, which stopped in the Paxos Zone during the Meocene-Pliocene period (5,5 million years ago), continues today, activating yet another plate which is several kilometres to the west and which results in earthquakes, many of which have proved catastrophic (such as that of 1953) for the Ionian Islands.

Geological phenomena

Cephalonia is notable for a number of peculiar geological and other phenomena, which have attracted the attention of scholars and scientists over the years, although no convincing explanations have yet been found for quite a number of them.

Lake Avythos, or Akoli, is in the district of Pyrgi, 50 kilometres from Argostoli. An old tradition held that it had no bottom (hence its name). Today its depth is known.

Kounopetra is a big rock in Pali, sticking out of the sea. It is located off the coast south of Lixouri, past the village of Mantzavinata. Once upon a time it was an internationally unique phenomenon, due to its ceaseless rhythmic movement. There is even a story that some British warships tied chains round it and hauled at it in an attempt to shift it, but without success. However, the earthquakes of 1953 managed, apart from destroying almost everything standing in Cephalonia, to stabilise the rock's bed, and now it does not move.

Another strange geological phenomenon of the island, the famous Katavothres, went unexplained for centuries. North of Argostoli at the entrance of its fine natural harbour, the seawater pours into two big rifts by the shore. Many efforts had been made to investigate this phenomenon, by pouring oil or dyes into the rifts. Still, no answer could be given and the 'mystery' remained. In 1963 a team of eminent Austrian geologists was more successful in their experiments. They poured a large amount of fluorescent dyes into one of the rifts, and two weeks later they located it off the coast of the bay of Sami, at Karavomylos, where brackish water streams into the sea. The scientific experiment was successfully repeated with the use of radio-isotopes and thus verified.

The Katavothres of Argostoli
1. The sea flows into the Katavothres at Argostoli
2. The sea water passes below the port of Argostoli and the mountains of the island.
3. Rain water.
4. The sea water and the rain water combine and continue their course eastwards at a much faster pace.
5. The brackish waters rise and emerge from the lagoon of Melissani and at Karavomylos, Fridi and Ayia Evfimia, Sami.

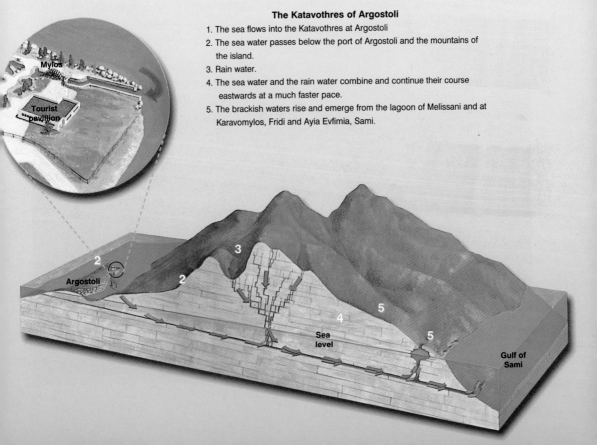

Natural Environment

Flora: The island has typical Mediterranean vegetation, with widespread shrubbery, held in check by holly bushes (Quercus coccifera) amongst which grow wild olive trees (Olea europaea subsp. oleaster), *turpentine trees* (Pistacia terbinthus), *mastich trees* (Pistacia lentiscus), *Spanish Broom* (Spartium junceum), *spiny broom* (Calicotome villosa), *arbutus* (Arbutus unedo), *wild arbatus* (Arbatus adrachne) *and many other species belonging to the so-called Mediterranean maquis. In some areas, the shrubbery has almost become a true forest, as the holly bushes have grown and become true trees. The thousands of goats that graze freely all over the island and in the spring eat the tender new shoots of the vegetation put a stop to this however.*

True forests exist on the hills of Mts Ainos and Roudi, where the Greek fir, known as Abies cephalonica, *grows. This type grows on all the tall mountains of central and southern Greece. We also find small forests with pine trees* (Pinus halepensis), *such as around Assos, whilst in* some areas there are forests with cypress trees (Cupresses sempervirens), *such as in the northern part of the island. The flora of Cephalonia is especially rich, and consists of thousands of species of plant. On Mt Ainos there are also a few endemic species, such as the* Saponaria aenesia, *the* Poa cephalonia, *the* Ajuga orientalis subsp. aenesia, *the* Scutellaria rubicunda subsp. cephalonica, *and the extremely rare and threatened species* Viola cephalonica, *which grows on the tallest peaks. Other species endemic to the island are the* Silene cephallenia, *which grows in the small ravine of Poros, and the* Limonium damboldtianum, *which lives in the coastal areas. Many other plants on the island are endemic to Greece; that is, they grow both in Cephalonia and many other parts of Greece. Such species are the* Arenaria guicciardii, *the* Paronychia albanica subsp. graeca, *the* Petrorhagia fasciculata, *the* Petrorhagia graminea, *the* Cerastium illyricum, *the* Dianthus fruticosus subsp. occidentalis, *the* Erysimum cephalonicum, *the* Astragalus cephalonicus, *the* Euphorbia zahnii, *the* Geocaryum

1

2 peloponnesiacum, *the* Scaligeria moreana, *the* Scaligeria moreana, *the* Campanula garganic subsp. cephallenica, *the* Stachys ionica, *the* Heptaptera colladonioides, *the* Stachys parolonii, *the* Teucrium halacsyanum, *the* Thymus holosericeus, *the* Crocus hadriaticus, *the* Serapias neglecta subsp. ionica, *the* Crocus boryi, *and the* Silene ungeri. *Other rare and interesting plants are the* Paeonia mascula subsp. russi, *which grows on Mt Ainos and at Roudi, the* Hypericum aegyptium, *which grows on the coastal rocks, the* Leucojum valentium, *which grows in the autumn, and the* Antirrhinum 3 siculum. *Common plants which can be found all over during the spring are the* Crepis rubra, *the* Papaver apulum, *the* Papaver rhoeas, *the* Malcolma maritima, *various plants of the genera* Vica *and* Lathyrus, *sorrel (*Oxalis pescaprae*), spurges (*Euphorbia rigida *and* Euphorbia characias*), the* Hypericum perfoliatum, *rock roses (*Cistus creticus *and* Cistus salvifolius*), bindweeds (*Convolvulus arvensis, Convolvulus alteheoides, Convolvulus elegantissumus*), red valerian (*Centranthus ruber*), camomile (*Anthemis chai*) the crown 4 daisy (*Chyrsanthemum coronarium*), asphodels (*Asphodelus aestivus*), hyacinths (*Muscari neglectum *and* Muscari comosum*) and many others. There are less flowering plants during the autumn, but these are still impressive. These include the sowbread (*Cyclamen hederifolium*), the* Crocus boryi, *the* Crocus hadriaticus, *the common sternbergia (*Sternbergia lutea*) and crocuses (*Colchicum sfikasianum, Colchicum cupanii, Colchicum haynaldii*). Mention must also be made of the various orchids of Cephalonia. Forty-four types have so far been found on the island, of the genera* Ophrys, Orchis, Serapias *and others.*

1. *View of Ainos with the Greek fir Abies cephalonica and the Mediterranean maquis.*
2. *Crocus hadriaticus, an endemic plant which flowers in the spring on the slopes of Mt Ainos.*
3. *Campanula garganica Cephallonica.*
4. *Spartium junceum (Spanish Broom).*

Fauna: The fauna of Cephalonia is not rich in mammals. The largest land animal is the fox, followed by the hare, the ferret and the hedgehog. The most important of the sea mammals is the rare Mediterranean monk seal (Monachus monachus) which is under threat of extinction. These seals nest in the caves on the isolated coasts of the island. There is also the loggerhead sea turtle (Caretta caretta), which can be found in the region of Kamnia, at the village of Ratzakli. As for birds, there is a significant presence of birds of prey, such as the long-legged buzzard (Buteo rufinus), the lesser kestrel (Falco naumanni), the kestrel (Falco tinnunculus), and others.

Other migratory or visiting birds of prey can also often be observed, such as the golden eagle (Aquila chrysaetos), Bonelli's eagle (Hieraetus fasciatus) and the peregrine (Falco peregrinus). There are also visiting vultures, such as the griffin vulture (Gyps fulvus) from neighbouring Aitolia.

Many mountain birds nest in the forests around Ainos, such as the black woodpecker (Dryocopus martius). In Ainos there also lives a small herd of wild horses of a local breed.

In 1956 the National Park of Ainos was founded in order to protect that wildlife of Cephalonia. The core of the National Park includes the main section of the fir tree forest and the neighbouring Mt Roudi. Currently, there is no peripheral zone around the park. Entrance to the National Park is free, although woodcutting, hunting, grazing, the gathering of plants and any other activity that may harm the natural environment is prohibited.

1. *Bee-eater.*
2. *Mediterranean Monk Seal.*
3. *Wild horses in the Ainos National Park.*

Small Wonders

The Greek and international mass media have on numerous occasions devoted space to the phenomenon of the snakes at Markopoulos, a village in the south-east of the island. The snakes, which are small and harmless, usually appear around the middle of August and, according to accounts published in the past, move freely through the streets of the village, in the direction of the church. They wriggle up to the silver icon of the Panayia (the Virgin) and disappear at the end of the service. Nowadays, the villagers collect them in glass vessels when they emerge from their hiding places and put them on the bishop's throne. At the end of the service they are released and promptly disappear. The locals call them 'the Panayia's snakes' and regard them as holy, their appearance being a good omen for the course of matters on the island. In order to support their claim that the snakes are holy, they point out the small black cross on the snakes' heads.

Another story records that these snakes first appeared in another church on the island, at the Panayia of Arginia. Another church, at Demoutsandata, is notable for a lily which, though withered all year, flowers in front of the icon of the Panayia during the church feast day on 23 August. Two more strange Cephalonian phenomena pertain to the animal kingdom. The historian Ioannis Kosti Loverdos notes a phenomenon which local inhabitants will confirm: some of the goats which graze on Mt Ayia Dinati, and some of the wild hares found there, would appear to have gold and silver teeth! Strange as this may sound, there is a scientific explanation for it. The soil in the Ayia Dinati area contains a number of substances which give the animals' teeth a gold or silver appearance.

The second peculiar animal phenomenon is the fact, noted even in ancient times by the sophist and historian Claudius Aelianus, that the goats of Cephalonia are able to go for as much as six months without drinking water and are able to sustain themselves by inhaling the damp breezes of the island. Even to this day, there are goatherds who affirm that from October to May they do not have to water their flocks.

The 'Panayia's snakes' in the church of the Panayia at Agrinia.

HISTORY

Mythology

A very ancient myth is connected with the name of the island. The myth tells of Cephalus (possibly a blend of two other mythical personages, one of them a son of Diomede and Dnion or Deioneas, and the other a son of Erse or Creousa with Hermes or Pandion). Cephalus was unresponsive to a declaration of love by the goddess Io and, in order to avenge herself upon him, the goddess caused Cephalus to suspect his wife Prokris of infidelity. Following Io's advice, Cephalus disguised himself and came before Prokris with rich gifts, managing to make her his concubine. When he revealed his true identity, Prokris fled in grief.

Prokris took refuge in Crete, where King Minos fell in love with her. To make her his, he gave her a dog which could run very fast and a spear which never missed its mark. But Prokris was afraid of the revenge which Minos' wife might take, and she returned to Athens. Artemis helped Prokris to regain the love and trust of Cephalus. When she learned of her husband's escapade with Io, she was overcome with jealousy and began to stalk him. Once when Cephalus was out hunting, Prokris concealed herself in the foliage of a bush so that he would not see her. Cephalus saw the branches moving and thought that it was a game animal. He therefore shot an arrow into the bush and killed his wife. Inconsolable, he exiled himself from Attica and went far away. He helped King Amphitryon defeat the Teleboans and the Taphians, and won his liking and gratitude. As a reward for his assistance, Amphitryon gave him the island, which then took his name (Cephalinia and later Cephalonia).

The myths involving Io can be seen on numerous vase paintings. The goddess is usually depicted with wings, driving a chariot drawn by two or four horses. In some other depictions, she holds the horses by the reins and runs in front of Helios. Most of the scenes in which she is represented show her with Cephalus or other lovers, and she is also associated with the killing of Memnon by Achilles.

Prehistory

The island is rich in prehistoric remains, especially funerary offerings (many of which are considered the only examples of their kind in the world) walls, and other buildings, and these indicate that there are strong grounds for believing that Cephalonia was inhabited considerably before 4000 BC. Indeed, there are some scholars who claim the first traces of human settlement on Cephalonia go back as far as the tenth millennium BC. At the end of 1984, Dr George V. Kavadias, a professor at the University of Athens, published his book 'Palaiolithiki Kefalonia'. This work brought to light many exceptional and significant facts about the prehistory of the island.

Above: depiction of Cephalus on a lekythos (480 BC).
Opposite: Io and Memnon on an early 5th-century cup
(Paris, Louvres).

Professor Kavadias detected traces of very ancient Palaeolithic civilisations in various areas of the island (Fiskardo, Mounta, Skala, Ai-Yorgis, Poros, the Argostoli peninsula, Spilio, Sami and elsewhere).

His finds are most impressive: a crowbar, double-bladed hand-axes, axes, choppers, cleavers, arrow-heads (in large, medium, and small sizes), 'backed' blades, wedged blades, scrapers of various shapes and sizes, chisels, awls, etc. Professor Kavadias writes that Fiskardo man seems to be similar to the one who created the neolithic civilisations of Southern Italy, the Western Peloponnese and Epirus.

He writes specifically:

"The Fiskardo finds belong to the Mousterian period. Their exact and accurate dating is not possible at this point, since no excavation has been carried out, and no geological strata with finds *in situ* have as yet been determined, especially in combination with plant and animal fossils, bones, traces of fire, etc., which would make possible the use of conventional dating methods (stratigraphy, palaeobotany, palaeontology, paleoanthropology, radio isotopes of potassium argon, carbon-14, etc.).

What can be soundly inferred today, on the basis of the available morphological comparative data, is that the Fiskardo finds can be placed to around 50,000 BC.

When the research is completed that dating may come close to or go beyond 80,000 BC."

The fact of the matter is that during the era of the Trojan War (Late Mycenean Period) Cephalonia had a quite developed level of civilisation. The islanders are not named as a separate people in the oldest parts of the 'Odyssey', although the islands of Dolichion, Sami and Hylessa are mentioned.

Scholars are fairly sure that the name 'paipaloessa Samos' (glittering Samos) refers to the main mountain chain of Cephalonia, and that Dolichion, according to ancient and modern scholars, was a part of the same island (possibly the Palic Peninsula). Homer also states that Dolichion was a fertile area, home of 52 of Penelope's suitors. There is another ancient tradition that Odysseus was a descendant of Cephalus.

Prehistoric finds from Fiskardo and Lakithra.

Antiquity

During the ancient period, the island was divided into four regions, each ruled by one city, making up the so-called 'Cephalonian tetrapolis'. The four cities were Sami, Pronnoi, Krani and Pali, the most important of which seems to have been Sami, which ruled the northern half of the east side of the island. Pali occupied the western peninsula (which today is known as the Palic Peninsula), and was an ideal staging post for communications between Corinth and Syracuse. Pronnoi extended over the south eastern edge of the island, and Krani ruled the western slopes of Mt Ainos.

The gods worshipped in Cephalonia were those of Olympus, of course, and especially Zeus, Demeter, Apollo, Poseidon, Dionysus, Herakles, Athena and Artemis. Temples and altars were built, sacrifices were made and ceremonies carried out. Near the highest peak of Mt Ainos was a famous sanctuary of Ainios or Ainissios Zeus, mentioned by Hesiod and dating back to the earliest times. Remains of it can be seen today, a little to the east of and below the summit. There is also a tradition that the small rocky islet of Dia, off the south coast, was also a famous holy site with a sanctuary dedicated to Zeus.

The climb to the peak of Mt Ainos is described with great lyricism by the 19th-century traveller D. Ansted, who notes the following:

" If we look in the direction of Argostoli, a small dot will be visible out in the ocean. Despite its size, this tiny islet, called Dios, was once the site of a temple dedicated to the father of the Gods. When a sacrifice was being offered up there, the smoke was visible to the priests at the altar of the temple on the peak of Ainos, and another sacrifice was made there too. The clouds of incense spiralling up from this high point through the thin air were a sign to all that the sacrifice had been concluded... "

In the third year of the 48th Olympiad (582 BC) the Pythian Games were organised at Delphi with much splendour and with the participation of athletes from all over the Greek world. In that year, the cithara (a form of ancient guitar) and flute competitions were added to the Games. The cithara competition was won by Melampus the Cephalonian. From this it is possible to judge

Coin from Krani (480-431 BC).

the degree to which music (and rhapsody) must have flourished on the island at that time.

Information about the political situation and policy directions taken by the tetrapolis is scarce for much of the classical and later periods. We know that Cephalonia took part in the Persian Wars along with the other Greeks. The four city-states followed and supported both sides during the Peloponnesian War. As was natural from its situation on the trade routes, Pali sided with Corinth, while Krani made an alliance with Athens. However, when the second Athenian League was initially formed (375 BC), Pronnoi and Pali were the only cities on the island to state their intention of joining. It is a fact that the different policies of the four city-states in antiquity often upset the general peace and prosperity of the island.

When Philip V of Macedonia besieged Pali in 218 BC, threatening to occupy and subject the whole of Cephalonia, all four cities joined the Aitolian League, which was fighting against Philip, and Pali was the only city to fight Philip's army. New conquerors arrived for good in 187 BC, when the Romans occupied the island, a little after their conquest of the rest of Greece. Of the four cities, Sami decided to resist, and indeed did so heroically, holding out for a four-month siege, after which the town was obliged to surrender and undergo the destruction and decimation of its population.

The Roman Period

Life in Cephalonia was undoubtedly difficult during the years of Roman occupation, what with maladministration and greed on the one hand and pirate raids on the other. About 50 BC, the whole island was the estate of Gaius Antonius, and a Kranian coin from the time of Augustus with the name and head of Gaius Proculius has been found. At about the beginning of the 2nd century AD, Cephalonia was given to Athens as a gift by the Emperor Poplius Aelius Hadrian, an admirer of Athens.

It would also appear that somewhat later, under the Antonines, the island enjoyed a brief spell of prosperity, especially in the region of Sami. This is confirmed by an honorary inscription in which the Samians refer with respect to the Emperor Septimius Severus.

Byzantium (330 - 1185)

Life in Cephalonia for the common man during the Byzantine period can have been no less unpleasant than it was under the Romans; the administration did not become any better, and the pirates continued to wreak destruction.

In the treatise 'Synekdemos' written by Hierocles before AD 535, Cephalonia is referred to among the 64 eparchies and 935 cities which recognised the authority of the Byzantine Emperor. Later, in the 10th century, the Emperor Constantine Porphyrogenetos wrote a treatise entitled 'Peri Thematon' ('Concerning the Themes'), in which he dealt with the major administrative divisions of the Empire (a 'theme' was one of the 31 administrative districts into which the Byzantine Empire was divided). The Emperor refers to Cephalonia as a theme which

1

also included the remaining Ionian Islands, with the exception of Kythera and possibly Zakynthos, which may have belonged to the theme of Greece.

Porphyrogenetos attributes the formation of the independent theme of Cephalonia to his grandfather Leo VI the Wise. The lead seals of some of the theme's officials have survived. There is also evidence that before the formation of an independent theme, Cephalonia and Zakynthos were detached from the Eparchy of Achaia and included in the 11th theme, that of Longobardia.

1. *Roman mosaic from Skala with a depiction of wild animals.*
2. *Interior of the church of Ayios Andreas at Petrata.*
3. *Exhibition room of the Corgialenios Historical and Folk Museum with exhibits from the Byzantine era.*

The Franks (1185 - 1194) - Venetian Rule (1194 - 1797)

In 1082, the men of the Norman baron Robert Guiscard landed on the island. They met stiff resistance from the Cephalonians, who formed resistance bands in various parts of the island. Guiscard, who was advanced in years, died of a fever in 1085 on board his ship anchored off Athera, in a bay near the port, thus giving his name, in a corrupted form, to the town Fiskardo.

Soon after this the Cephalonians and the inhabitants of the other Ionian Islands experienced at first hand the revenge of another Norman, the nobleman Bohemund. Whilst on his way back from one of the Crusades, he sacked the Ionian Islands with the greatest of cruelty, as a punishment for Guiscard's 'failure'. In 1147, the islands were occupied by Normans once more, although the Byzantine Emperor Manuel, with the help of the Venetians, managed to drive them out again.

But in 1158 he was forced to sign a peace treaty which effectively handed the islands over to the Norman baron Roger I.

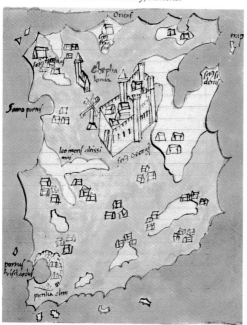

Painting of Cephalonia on wood,
Gennadios Library, Athens.

The process of separation from the Byzantine Empire was completed in 1185, with the formation of the Palatine Duchy of Cephalonia and Zakynthos, under William II and the Norman crown, with the pirate admiral Margaritone (or Megariti) of Brindisi as first overlord. He was succeeded in 1194 by Matthios Orsini. With the Frankish occupation of Constantinople (1204), Cephalonia was confirmed in Orsini's name under the sovereignty of Venice.

Orsini bears various names in the Latin texts in which he is mentioned (Mahius, Madius, Gallus, Gallicus, and so on), while the 'Chronicle of the Morea', a principal source for this period, has him as Count Maios. Whatever his exact name, he used Cephalonia as a base and cover for various piratical activities, including co-operation with the brutal Leo Vetrano of Genoa, his formal allegiance to the Norman King of Sicily not withstanding.

This was the time at which the power and influence of the Vatican over political and military affairs in Europe was increasing, and Orsini eventually clashed with papal interests.
At first, he was able to pull the wool over the Vatican's eyes with false confessions of repentance, but soon he was forced to 'cede' the Cephalonia-Zakynthos Palatinate to Pope Innocent III. Having, as it thought, got what it wanted, the Vatican proceeded to forget all the pressure and blackmail it had subjected Orsini to, and began to hail him in its letters as 'noble man', 'Our most worthy son', and so on. Needless to say, the crafty pirate had no intention whatever of simply handing over to the Pope an enterprise which had proved so profitable, and indeed he managed, while keeping on the best of terms with the Pope and his agents, to exercise power just as he had done before, to his own great personal benefit. This led the Vatican to put its own schemes into action once more.

In a letter of 15 September 1207, Pope Innocent II grants forgiveness to 'the Count of the islands of Cephalonia and Zakynthos', and conveys his blessings to the Cephalonians 'and his other subjects'. At the same time, he abolished the Orthodox bishoprics of Cephalonia and Zakynthos and ordered that the Western rite be officially recognised and established.

By 1209, Orsini had come to the conclusion that perhaps an alliance with the Venetians would be more in his interests. Thus he surrendered his islands to the suzerainty of the Most Sublime Republic of Venice. The Vatican boiled with rage, but the pirate was able to calm the Pope and his minions down somewhat with a promise of a substantial payment in tribute each year. Of course, in this, as in other matters, no one thought of asking the people of Cephalonia (or Zakynthos) what they felt about the question or as to whether, on top of all the other taxes and tributes they paid - not to mention the sums lost to pirate activity - they felt like subsidising the Pope as well.

The Pope and his people continued their games of power politics, ordering Orsini to sail with eight galleys and a force of men to Egypt to fight at the side of the King of Jerusalem. This resulted in a show of anger on the part of King Frederick II of Sicily, who ordered that Orsini's estates in Apulia should be confiscated, a threat which was only averted with the personal intervention of the Pope. A little prior to this, in 1216, Orsini had promised to pay the Vatican treasury 50 gold pieces each year. On the eastern front, too, Orsini was extremely concerned to maintain good relations with the Despot of Epirus, Theodore Angelos Comnenos. As can be seen from two surviving letters of Benedict, Roman Catholic Bishop of Cephalonia, Orsini entered into and encouraged a number of marriages of convenience with the ruling house of Epirus and Thessaloniki which would ensure for himself and his family tenure in the islands. However, the Despotate of Epirus was a short-lived affair, broken up by Bulgarian invasion after a welter of plots, poisonings, marriages and succession struggles. Cephalonia and Zakynthos now came under the Villehardouins, nobles of Achaia, and strong links were formed between the islands and Achaia. A report by the united Latin bishopric of Cephalonia and Zakynthos, dated 1264, is a rich source of information about this period, and especially about the possessions of the Church and Cephalonian place-names. Most of these are Greek in origin, although there is often a Frankish (European) influence. Only a few are derived from other languages. Place-names, ending in -ata or -ades denote settlements originally founded by Frankish colonists. For example, we have Ferentinata (in Pylaros, a Florentine colony), Karousata (founded by the Caruso family of Naples), Monopalata (on the Palic peninsula, settlers from Monopoli in Apulia), Solomata (from the Venetian Solomos family), Bekatorata (from the Milanese family of Becatoros), and so on.

In the meantime, there was continued and merciless in fighting between the various lordlings of the area - a characteristic trait of the Frankish rulers of the era. The second son of the original Orsini was succeeded, in his turn, by his own son John I. He, in order to consolidate his position still further, married Maria, daughter of the despot Nikephoros of Epirus and sister of the last Greek despot, Thomas Comnenos. John I's successor, Thomas-Nikolaos, first ceded the lordship of Cephalonia and Zakynthos to his brother John II. He then murdered his uncle Thomas Comnenos, converted to Orthodoxy and usurped the throne of Epirus. John II was hardly any better. He murdered his usurping brother and kept the throne of Epirus for himself. He also converted to Orthodoxy, hellenised his name to Ioannis-Angelos Comnenos and married Anna Palaiologos (of the ruling family in Byzantium). She seems to have been possessed of even more ambition than her husband, for she had him poisoned.

Thus the line of the Orsinis died out, and there were no more Palatine Counts of Cephalonia and Zakynthos.The islands passed into the hands of Sicilian princes. Ioannis-Angelos Comnenos had recognised the suzerainty of King Philip I of Naples over the Duchy of Cephalonia and Zakynthos. Philip's first son,Robert, who succeeded his father, was defeated and taken prisoner in battle, and his escape from Germany was aided by the brothers Leonardo, Petro and Luigi de Tocchi. As a show of gratitude, Robert granted the Tocchi family the islands of Cephalonia, Zakynthos and Ithaki, and gave his sister Francesca in marriage to the new Leonardo I (1357). A few years later, in 1362, Lefkada and Vonitsa were added to the Tocchi possessions.

The Tocchi line produced five 'Dukes of Lefkada, Counts of Cephalonia and Masters of

Vonitsa', and from time to time their rule extended over other parts of central Greece and the Peloponnese. Leonardo I was exceptional in that his stance towards the local people tended toward the friendly, and he made a sincere effort to put the semi-ruined islands back on their feet again. This policy, however, was cut short by his successor, Carlo I, who returned to the old pattern of the belligerent, rapacious, greedy and violent ruler to whom the Cephalonians had grown accustomed over the centuries. Carlo made a marriage alliance with the Duchy of Athens by marrying Francesca Acciaioli and this, together with some military operations, brought him control over Arta, Akarnania, Glarentza, and some other parts of the hinterland of Achaia and Albania.

It was precisely this extension of power which brought the Cephalonians their only respite or relief during the years of Carlo's reign, for his increased strength removed the tributes which had been paid to the lords of Achaia. And towards the end of Carlo's life, when he had left the administration of the Duchy in the hands of his brother Leonardo II, there was a definite change for a little while, at least.

Carlo I finally died in 1429, and was succeeded by his nephew, Carlo II, who was declared "By the Grace of God, Lord of Arta, Duke of Lefkada, Count Palatine of Cephalonia, Ithaki and Zakynthos". The new lord was able, for a few years, to keep his peace both with the Italians and the Turks. His son Leonardo III, who succeeded in 1448, was also able, with the help and protection of the Venetians, to keep the principality intact, even managing to keep a foothold on the mainland at Vonitsa.

The castle of Ayios Georgios, from the Anville collection.

Zuritas, a Spanish historian of the time, records that in his day Cephalonia had two harbours, 15,000 houses and about 40,000 inhabitants. Leonardo III married Militsa, grand-daughter of Thomas Palaiologos, in 1463.

A few years before this, in 1452, he had re-established the bishopric of the Orthodox Church in Cephalonia, while at the same time ensuring that the Catholic Bishopric of Cephalonia and Zakynthos would continue to enjoy its privileges. Leonardo III moved his palace from Lefkada to the Castle of Ayios Georgios, which had been built in a fortified position above Livatho and Kranaia in Cephalonia.

In the meantime, the Turks had been gradually taking over the Greek world dafter the fall of Constantinople in 1453. The Ionian Islands were among the prizes they valued most, and Leonardo III was forced to give battle, sometimes victoriously and sometimes resulting in peace treaties which compelled Venice to pay the Turks an annual tribute. The Turks first landed on the island in 1479. Antonio Tokkos, brother of Leonardo, attempted with the help of the local populace and the Venetians to throw out the conquerors, but failed, and was put to death by his local supporters.

In 1500, the Venetians, aided by Spain, laid siege to the Castle of Ayios Georgios and captured it, slaughtering the Turkish garrison. Cephalonia became once more a major way-station for Venetian ships.

But the Turks did not give up so easily. In 1538 they raided the island, taking away with them 13,000 Cephalonians as slaves.

In the 18th century, fighting broke out between the powerful families, each of which was helped by armed bands of supporters. Thus the Aninos family fought the Metaxas family, the Karoussos family drew the sword against the Antypas family, the Typaldos family was at daggers drawn with the Loverdos family, and so on. It was difficult in these

The entrance to the castle of Ayios Georgios at Assos.

Demographic Growth of Cephalonia (1548 - 1655)			
Year	No. of inhabitants	Year	No. of inhabitants
1548	14.000	1583	24.755
1569	24.392		(along with Ithaki)
	(along with Ithaki)	1587	25.000
1572	18.200	1601	30.828
1576	19.000	1608	39.591
1580	20.000	1620-1635	50.000
1582	22.000	1655	60.000

conditions to maintain peaceful conditions and the island's prosperity fell. In the end, the Venetian authorities were forced to take drastic measures, arresting the ring-leaders and taking them to Venice, where they were hanged.

In 1757 the seat of the governor ('Provleptis') was transferred from the castle of Ayios Georgios to Argostoli, which was already an important urban centre.

The period of Venetian rule ended in 1797, with the dissolution of the 'Most Serene Republic of Venice' by Napoleon and the French army's invasion of the Ionian Islands.

French, British, Russo - Turkish Rule

French rule (1797-1798)

The people of Cephalonia received with enthusiasm and excitement the news that the French fleet had sailed into Corfu, on 28 June 1797. General Gentili, as representative of Napoleon, issued a proclamation to the people of the Ionian Islands promising that the French forces would liberate all the islands in the group and would help Greece to regain her ancient glory.

The 'Libro d' Oro' (golden book) with the names of the Ionian nobility was burned publicly amid general rejoicing. Between laughter and tears the Cephalonians sang the revolutionary songs of Rigas Velistenlis, and news spread back and forth throughout the Ionian Islands of the celebrations that were taking place. Some of the more hot-blooded went so far as to attempt to attack members of the former nobility, but they were restrained by the calmer citizens and serious incidents were avoided.

The Treaty of Campo Formio (17 October 1797) made full recognition of French rights over the islands, and on 1 November of the same year their annexation to the French state was announced. For administrative purposes, they were divided into three prefectures.

The Russo-Turkish intervention (1798) and the 'Ionian State' (1800-1807)

The disaster which overcame the French fleet at the Battle of Abukir in 1798 led to an agreement between the Russians and the Turks - with British connivance - to take over the Ionian Islands as allies. The Russo-Turkish fleet, under Admiral Utsakof, occupied Kythera on 12 October 1798, and on 29 October anchored off Argostoli.

The Russo-Turkish regime revived the aristocratic system of administration which the French had abolished. A five-member government consisting of nobles was set up, and among its first acts was to send messages of congratulations to the Tsar, the Sultan and Admiral Nelson, who had been responsible for the defeat of the French at Abukir. The Russians soon gave way to Turkish pressure to cede to the Porte the sovereignty of the islands. The Treaty of Constantinople, signed on 21 March 1800, established the 'Ionian State' and brought the islands under sole Turkish suzerainty. According to the constitution of this, the ordinary people were once more deprived of all political rights. Each island was to be ruled by a Grand Council, which would exercise all administrative and judicial authority. The members of these Councils, were, of course, also members of the nobility, and it was clearly stated that they must be hereditary aristocrats. The people rose in revolt and there was a violent reaction on all the islands. In Cephalonia, revolutionaries occupied Argostoli. The Speaker of the Senate, Spyridon G. Theotokis, attempted to organise the election of an 'honourable representative body' of city-dwellers and farmers to draw up a new constitution, but this was not ratified by the Turkish government.

After the Treaty of Amiens (1802), and on the suggestion of Napoleon, the Russians sent to the Ionian Islands the Zakynthian Count George Mocenigo. He called elections, to return representatives of all classes of the people as senators and delegates to a constitutional assembly. These representatives, together with the Tsar's plenipotentiary, drew up and, on 23 December 1803, passed, a new constitution. This historic document abolished the hereditary aristocracy, established personal freedoms and was the first document of its kind to make official recognition of the modern Greek nation (Article 211). The same article of the Constitution established Greek as the official language of the state. To the new state was given the name 'Septinsular Republic' (in Greek the islands are also known as the 'Eptanisia', or 'seven islands').

The second period of French Rule (1807)

By the Treaty of Tilsit, in 1807, Tsar Alexander II of Russia ceded the Ionian Islands to France. General Bertier (later Prince of Neuvechatelle), as representative of the Emperor Napoleon, abolished the constitution of 1803 and proclaimed the Ionian Islands a province of France. But things did not go as well as the French had hoped. Napoleon replaced Bertier with General Donzeleau, who, in a proclamation issued on 10 November 1807, brought the 1803 Constitution of the Septinsular Republic back into force. The local inhabitants greeted the return of the French warmly. But the new period of peaceful occupation was to last only two years, for in 1809 Britain declared a blockade of the Ionian islands as part of the general war being undertaken against Napoleon. On 19 September 1809, three British frigates with 3,000 soldiers took the castle of Zakynthos and hoisted over it the British flag.

British rule (1809-1864)

Cephalonia, Ithaki and Kythera soon surrendered. In Cephalonia, as in the other islands, the British set up provisional governments. The other islands in the chain gave in over the next few years to the new masters, despite varying degrees of reaction from the pro-French groups. At the Congress of Vienna and with the Treaty of Paris of 1815 the Great Powers of the time cooked up various suggestions regarding the fate of the Ionian Islands. It was finally decided by Britain, Austria and Prussia (France and Turkey accepting later on) that a free and independent state should be formed, under the title 'United States of the Ionian Islands', yet with British 'protection'. This 'protection' amounted to the requirement that the constitution of the islands be submitted to the British Government for approval and the condition that the Ionian Islands would not have a right to separate diplomatic representation. They would, however, be able to receive consuls from other countries. The affairs of the islands were to be supervised by a Lord High Commissioner, who would represent the British throne.

One of the first governors of Cephalonia, the Swiss Charles-Philippe de Bosset, who served as a colonel in the British Army, was responsible for a number of useful major works on the island. The most important was the large stone bridge with many arches which linked Argostoli with the coast opposite.

In contrast with de Bosset, the first British Lord High Commissioner, Sir Thomas Maitland, made himself extremely unpopular with the islanders, owing to his despotic behaviour and high-handed administration. His Constitution was published on 28 December 1817, and it was immediately evident that it afforded the British authorities powers which amounted to absolute control over the island's affairs, depriving the citizens of any meaningful say in the way things were run.

The Cephalonians, just like the other Ionian islanders, reacted to the arbitrary and tyrannical rule which the Commissioner and other instruments of British Protection attempted to impose. At first, the Cephalonians created clandestine resistance groups and conspiracies. Later they manifested their opposition openly.

The 1821 War of Independence and attempts at unification with Greece

The people of Cephalonia made a significant contribution to the Greek War of Independence of 1821, and many of its leading citizens were members of the Society of Friends (Philiki Etaireia) which paved the way for and declared the outbreak of the Greek War of Independence. Among these were:

- Dimitrios Dalladetsimas, who was initiated into the Society by the Zakynthian Dionysios Romas. Under the British protectorate, Dalladetsimas rose to the upper levels of the judicial system, but this did not impede him from collecting money and stores for the fighters on the mainland, spreading the word among his fellow islanders and putting his house and wealth at the disposal of refugees from the war-torn areas and foreign philhellenes on their way to take part in the struggle.
- Dimitrios Corgialenios, who not only played an active part in sending food and supplies to mainland Greece and looking after refugees but fought in the War as well.
- The lawyer Gerasimos Livadas, who founded, in Argostoli, an association which was supposedly recreational but was in fact involved in the organisation and encouragement of the resistance.
- Spyridon Destounis, a legal expert and writer of history in Russia and Councillor of State to the Russian Empire; at the risk of his own life he managed to ship many of his compatriots to safety far from the wrath of the Turks.
- Gerasimos Koupas, sailor and mathematician. When Turkish anger broke loose and the slaughter of the Greeks of Constantinople began, he escaped in his ship and went to the island of Psara, where he made a gift of the ship to the locals.
- Georgios Kozakis Typaldos, a doctor who began his promising career with brilliant studies in Paris. He was very active in the countries around the Danube, spreading the influence of the Society of Friends and writing propagandistic patriotic books and plays.

Other Cephalonian members of the 'Sacred Band' founded by Ypsilantis include the brothers Anastasios and Nikolaos Inglesis, Spyridon Voutsinas, Dimitrios Choidas, Gerasimos Orfanos and Loukas Valsamakis, who commanded the third troop of the Band.

The battle of Lala was the climax of the patriotism, self-denial and heroism of the Cephalonians. The leading figures were Constantine and Andreas Metaxas, two eminent and creative members of the Society of Friends, who led the Cephalonian fighting units, along with Vangelis Panas and Gerasimos Fokas. The Cephalonian units joined up with some formations from the Peloponnese and marched on Lala, a village on Mt Pholoi, in Elia, the base of a group of wild and vicious Turko-Albanians (Muslim Albanians who fought for the Turks). The fighting lasted from 29 May to 22 June 1821. The village was finally taken on 24 June, after the Turks, along with the reinforcements sent by Yusuf Pasha, had abandoned it to the attackers.

In the later years of the Independence Struggle, too, the cousins Constantine and Andreas Metaxas, Vangelis Panas and Gerasimos Fokas, together with Daniel Panas, Dionysios Fokas and many others, continued to lead various units of the Greek forces, to offer themselves and their fortunes selflessly and to give all their strength for the country they wished to see free.

British administration to 1848

Colonel Sir Charles Napier was appointed Resident (military and civil commander) of Cephalonia in 1821. He and the engineer Kennedy, built roads and public buildings, which brought prosperity to the island, opening it up to communications and trade.

Among the buildings dating from the Napier period was the imposing colonnaded edifice constructed on the sea-front square at Lixouri in 1824 and popularly known as the 'Markato'. It was the first courtroom on the island, and its main hall could seat 600 people.

After the death of Lord High Commissioner Thomas Maitland, in 1824, the post passed to Frederick Adam, whose attitude to the islands and the way in which they should be ruled was much milder than that of his predecessor. Seven years later, in 1831, Lord Nugent, who was far more upright and a philhellene, took over. But retired general Howard Douglas, who ruled from 1835-41, caused a storm of popular criticism and outrage with his inhuman style of administration. It is noteworthy that during these years the Cephalonians avoided any contact with the British. However, relations were somewhat restored under the next Lord High Commissioner Stewart McKenzie (1841-3) and his successor John Seaton, who was particularly respected by the Ionian Islanders.

Revolutionary stirrings

The proclamation of the French Republic, on 25 February 1848, caused a wave of revolutionary fervour throughout Europe. The Cephalonians, with their liberal tradition, were not to be left behind, and began to organise themselves. A revolt broke out on 14 September 1848. Two hundred villagers took up arms and went down to Argostoli, where they clashed with British troops. More armed villagers entered Lixouri, but were forced to retire when British forces arrived from Argostoli. Seaton hurried to Cephalonia, where he granted an amnesty to the ring-leaders. A month later, a law was published granting freedom of the Press, the right to found associations and clubs, and freedom of assembly for the discussion of common problems.

Soon after this, the Radical Party was founded in Cephalonia. The initiators of the movement were inspired by the idea of uniting the islands with Greece: among them were Elias Zervos Iakovatos, Joseph Momferatos and Gerasimos Livadas. Another party formed at the same time, the Reformists, claimed that the time was not yet ripe for union with Greece and demanded the reform of the 1817 Constitution. In addition to these groupings, there were also a number of opportunists who had thrown in their lot with the British, founding the Conservative Party, which rejected the ideas of the other parties and supported a continuation of British control. The Conservatives were known as 'the Fiends'. Seaton was prepared to accept wide-ranging reforms of the 1817 Constitution, and

George Ward, who succeeded him in 1849, announced in the Ionian Parliament that Queen Victoria was prepared to ratify the reforms.

But the 'Fiends' provoked a new and bloody rising, whose aim was to create a climate of anarchy and force the British to suspend all the liberties they had granted. The rising was put down by Ward's troops and the ring-leaders mercilessly punished. At the same time, harsh measures against the same progressives, and especially the Radicals, were introduced, and Elias Zervos Iakovatos and Joseph Momferatos were exiled for a second time.

The first free Parliament (1850)

Nonetheless, the patriotic Cephalonians continued their activities undeterred, publishing newspapers, holding meetings, and submitting protests to all quarters. In the end, Queen Victoria was compelled to ratify the constitutional reforms, and thus free elections were held in 1850, to return members to what was called the Ninth Parliament, but was actually the first free one. In Cephalonia, the Radical candidates Elias Zervos Iakovatos, Joseph Momferatos, Gerasimos Livadas, Ioannis Typaldos Kapeletos, Ioannis Typaldos Dotoratos, George Typaldos and Stamatelos Pylarinos were elected. On 26 November 1850, Ioannis Typaldos Kapeletos rose in Parliament and began to read out a motion to the effect that Parliament proclaimed the wish of the people of the Ionian Islands for independence and unification with Greece, calling upon the European Powers to support this wish. However, the reading of the motion was never to finish, for at the end of the first paragraph the Speaker was handed an order from the Lord High Commissioner to suspend proceedings. More severe policing measures, prosecutions and exiles followed.

Photographs from the Corgialenios Historical and Folk Museum (1856-1906)
1. Markatos.
2. The stone-paved road to Krani.

Gladstone's efforts

In 1855, John Young took over as Lord High Commissioner, and attempted to moderate the poor impressions made by his harsh and unbending predecessors.

His efforts to install rational administration in the area were, however, made more difficult by an ever more intensive unification movement. William Gladstone, one of the most able of British politicians, was sent to the Ionian Islands in 1856 to report on the situation and see what could be done. The Philhellene Gladstone saw wherever he went that the desire of the islanders was for complete unification with Greece. In 1857 Young set free the exiled Radicals. Gladstone appeared before Parliament on 24 January - 5 February 1859, with a whole series of new constitutional amendments. But Parliament had been deceived many times before with similar offers and, when it came down to it, was not prepared to accept 'administration' by a foreign Power. It therefore rejected Gladstone's proposals and insisted upon the demand of union.

The last two Parliaments and unification

The eleventh Parliament was dissolved and the twelfth was in session from 15-27 February 1862. Elias Zervos Iakovatos and Joseph Momferatos were resoundingly chosen as Speaker and Deputy Speaker respectively. Meanwhile, the struggle for unification continued. In free Greece, political intrigue had led to the abdication of King Otho and the proclamation of Prince George of Denmark, the second son of Prince Christian, as King. The British Government judged that the moment had come for it to relinquish its 'protection' from the Ionian Islands. The other Powers agreed and the twelfth Parliament was dissolved in July 1863. The thirteenth and final Parliament met from 17-29 September of the same year and, on 23 September, passed a resolution calling for the union of the islands with Greece. This last Parliament was dissolved on 7 April 1864, and a few days later Thrasyboulos Zaimis, specially empowered by the Greek National Assembly, arrived in Corfu to take over the Ionian Islands from Lord High Commissioner Henry Storks. The official ceremony took place on 21 May 1864, and the islands were at last part of Greece.

Contemporary History

Detailed or specialised studies of the modern history of Cephalonia until the present day do not exist. A few specialised monographs have been published; however, they deal with a specific time-frame, personality or event. Usually, those who write about Cephalonia - several of them being local historians - either confine themselves to the vague sentence "Cephalonia's fate was similar to that of the other Ionian islands," or stop their historical survey on the date of the islands' official union with Greece. From two historical studies, located after considerable research, we have extracted some relevant data.

Historian Spyros D. Loukatos in his book Marinos S. Antypas, about the life, personality, struggles and times of the Cephalonian socialist fighter, who played a leading role in the Thessalian peasant uprising, has included information on that period. He writes:

"Just as in all the Ionian Islands, in Cephalonia the slow but steady process of assimilation to the political, social and economic establishment of the liberated mainland began in 1864, when the Ionian Islands became united with Greece. Even before unification, the island's old truly democratic Radical Movement had been altered in its essence and goals by the 'pseudo-radical' movements of the other islands. After union it became ineffective, owing due to its idle or conciliatory leadership; it went down in history as a popular movement which survived only thanks to its genuine descendants, such as Pan, Panas and Rocco Hoidas. Still, It had undergone changes, on account of the existing conditions in Greece and in Europe and had evolved in form and content to express the new democratic and social ideological tendencies. Cephalonia's unification with Greece and its gradual assimilation did not alter the situation which prevailed on the island during the period of British rule."

An event that marked the Ionian islands during World War II was the clash between Italians and Germans, when anti-Fascist Italian soldiers refused to turn over the command to the German invaders.

About this clash, which took place in September *1943 and in which thousands of lives were lost either on the battlefield or in the mass executions of Italian fighters, Spyros D. Loukatos writes in his account:*

"... it constitutes a very important feat of the common Greek-Italian anti-Fascist front, resisting the Italian-German Fascist one. It was one of the greatest accomplishments of the EAM's (National Liberation Front) National Resistance in the Ionian Islands, and particularly in Cephalonia. It was one of the most important anti-Fascist events anywhere in occupied Greece and a very dramatic one on the Mediterranean front during World War II, which led to the final collapse of Italian Fascism and Italy's capitulation."

1. The monument in honour of Panayis Vallianos at Keramies.
2. Bust of Ioannis Metaxas at Assos.

2

3

CULTURE AND TRADITION

People and occupations - Customs and Traditions
Arts and Letters - Architecture

Life in the towns and villages of Cephalonia today follows modern trends and habits.

The southern part of the island is the most developed, and the large towns and the hundreds of villages of Cephalonia are to be found here. Here, tourism and a lot of foreign habits encroach upon the island daily through the harbours and the airport.

Despite all this, some insist upon sticking to the old traditions. These are usually the older people who were raised according to a different way of life which it is not easy for them to give up. There are also those who live in the isolated villages far from the centre of the island, where the rhythms of a closed society lend themselves to the preservation of traditions.

Most times, however, such traditions are left behind by the passage of time. Even so, it is worth exploring them, even if for some they are nothing more than an interesting piece of encyclopaedic knowledge.

A piece of knowledge, however, which without any doubt shaped the reality of the island today.

The island's wisdom can only be discovered among those who stick to tradition...

The Cephalonians

The Cephalonians are cheerful, quick-witted, imaginative and always ready for a joke or some teasing. They are fond of self-satire, which takes the form of popular epigrammatic couplets; there is a long tradition of this on the island, and it has produced some notable poets: (Laskaratos, Avlichos, Anninos and others). The islanders say of themselves that they are a little 'crazy' - but this is a special kind of 'craziness' which fills them with pride, rather than a failing. They are cordial and hospitable towards the foreigners who visit their island, even though they consider themselves localists. In their social relations, the islanders are both courteous and pleasant. They are particularly notable for their hospitality and the delight they take in providing for their friends and acquaintances, and also for the strangers who visit their island and whom they have never met before.

A good description of the typical Cephalonian character is given by the painter and writer Diana Antonakatou in her study 'The Cephalonian

Woman' ('Eos' magazine, issue 58-60, 1962):

"The male character-type has established itself in the Greek mind: an islander with an individual, active and resourceful nature covered only by the term 'Cephalonian'. The term is associated with all sorts of jokes, anecdotes and stories of craftiness and guile to such an extent that the 'Cephalonian' in the popular mind is a separate figure from the other Ionian Islanders. One of the reasons for this is that the Cephalonians were the most travelled of the island peoples.

"Within the context of the common fate of the islands, the geological peculiarities of Cephalonia - bare, infertile and untameable - and of its geographical position - furthest from the Greek mainland - the Cephalonian reacted differently during the long social evolution of the Ionian Islands. He is more ready to take up arms and fight during the great hours of social and national conflicts. He is less liable to succumb to slavery during lengthy foreign occupation. His drive to live is stronger, and this has taken him out into the wide world. He is much more practical, of course. And above all, 'migratory'."

1, 2. Traditional dress of different periods at the Corgialenios Historical and Folk Museum. Opposite: engravings showing traditional Cephalonian dress.

The Siora and the Cephalonian Woman of the Plain

"The 'Siora', the Cephalonian woman of the aristocratic class, would always speak Italian at home, wear European clothes designed according to the height of fashion, and would have been brought up in the European style from her earliest days. However much her position may have been subordinate to that of her husband, she had a relative degree of independence and a certain social freedom for her time. And, of course, she had nothing in common with the treatment of women as slaves, in accordance with the Turkish ideal, as practised in the other Greece. For her there were no bars on the windows, and her face did not have to be covered. The 'Siores' were to be found in each others' houses, at dances, and later at the theatre, which became their main form of entertainment. The middle class, which developed more slowly, and which was always bourgeois in mentality, naturally took the aristocracy as its model. Of course, it could not teach its daughters Italian and music or prepare them for a leading role in society, since it did not even have the means to advance its sons. But the daughters of the middle class were nonetheless brought up to behave less slavishly and obediently. They would wear European clothes, but never, not even in recent years, would they dare to appear in a hat, as the 'ladies' did."

Further on, Ms Antonakatou writes:

"With the passage of time, the aristocratic Cephalonian lady acquired more and more personal freedom and a more liberated attitude towards the lower classes. This helped give all three classes a certain number of points in common. The poor Cephalonian women may have tried to emulate the appearance and manners of their rich counterparts, but whether she liked it or not, the rich woman would also acquire some of the habits and abilities of the village or working-class woman. Speech, the method of communication, was more or less the same for all classes, the only difference being that the language used by the people was richer in expression and individuality, since it attempted to make the foreign influences submit to native Greek plasticity."

"...The Cephalonian village woman, whether she lived on the plains or in the mountains, or in Lixouri, Sami, Poros or Thinia, was of course the hardest done-by, in terms of the means available to her, the amount of work she was required to do and the struggle to live. All the other women of the other classes may have boasted about their housekeeping abilities, their good manners and their hospitable intentions, their readiness for action and their ability to take the initiative. But they did not have to experience the hard life on the land. The Cephalonian village woman did not live in the slavery borne by so many other Greek village women. Nonetheless, there was no part of the farm work which did not involve her: the field work, the vineyard, the olives, bringing up the children and the housework. She, too, had a corner of which she could be proud. But although the lessons she took from the aristocrat taught her much, they were quick to deprive her of her picturesque local dress".

"According to K.F. Kosmetatos, in his book Kefallinika, the traditional rural costume started to die out in the mid-nineteenth century. It was so simple anyway and already displayed European elements... The Cephalonian village woman stopped using the loom, as she opted for ready-made clothes".

Diana Antonakatou, 'The Cephalonian Woman'
('Eos' magazine, issue 58-60, 1962)

Occupations

From ancient times, Cephalonia's economy was based upon agriculture, its use as a commercial trade route, and shipping. With the passage of the centuries, however, commercial trade became properly organised and was no longer dependent upon the bravery and instinct of the sailors, such as that of the Cephalonians. The island's importance as a trade route thus became secondary and the main source for the economy during the years 1864-1940 remained **agriculture,** the nature of which was determined by the kind of land-holdings, where large land-holdings and monastery possessions dominated. This created the 'tenant-farmer system'. The main agricultural products were: extraquality olive oil, aromatic early strawberries, citrus fruits, wine, grapes, honey, nuts, garden vegetables, herbs and herbal teas.

The Cephalonians even specialised in certain sweets, such as nougat, 'mantoles', rozolia and others.

Alongside this, they began to establish small industries, such as flour mills, pasta production, wineries, leather processing, etc. The great political and social upheavals in the rest of Europe and the world did not leave Cephalonia untouched. At the end of the 19th century, then, another source of wealth - migration - appeared which, on the one hand deprived the island of manpower, but, on the other hand, provided it with a cash inflow. During the same period, there was an increase in the number of people involved with **trade** and **shipping.** This cash inflow and the development of shipping led to the foundation on the island of the first insurance company, 'Archangelos', which later evolved into a large shipping bank with its base in London. On 10 August 1840, a branch of the Ionian Bank, the first bank in Greece, the headquarters of which were on Corfu, was opened on Cephalonia.

Scenes from the daily lives of the locals.

The sea-faring tradition and an unusual Cephalonian

The sea-faring and emigration traditions in Cephalonia go back a very long way. Many islanders have acquired considerable fortunes at sea and have become major benefactors of the community, making large gifts and undertaking other creative initiatives (building churches and other edifices destroyed by the earthquake, founding hospitals and other institutions). One of the cases which stands out in the Cephalonian sea-faring tradition is that of Constantine Yerakis (1647-1688).

He left home at the age of only 13 and ran away to sea, enlisting on an English ship as a deck-hand. He later became an employee of the British East India Company. Settling in India, he became a scholar of the languages and customs of the Indian sub-continent and of the other peoples of the East. His cleverness and commercial talent, combined with his knowledge of languages, enabled him to amass a huge fortune. But a shipwreck sent most of his wealth to the bottom of the sea. By a happy chance, the ship which sank was also being used as transport by a messenger from the King of Siam, and Yerakis took good care of him after the wreck. The ambassador invited Yerakis to come to Siam, and presented him to the King, who was so impressed by the clever and hard-working Cephalonian that he made him Prime Minister of the country and Regent! Yerakis protected the Catholic Church in Siam, organised the state finances and cultivated close commercial relations with France and England. But the Portuguese and Dutch, competitors of the French and English, encouraged the court officials to revolt, deposing and executing both the King and his Regent. Yerakis' Siamese wife Maria (and, according to one source, his son) were also put to death.

These new developments and the movement of the population into new forms of employment resulted in the creation of new social classes, the strengthening of radicalism, and the development of the island's intellectual and cultural life. At the same time a new activity and source of wealth, with all its repercussions, began to make its presence felt on the island: tourism.

All this was cut short with the catastrophic earthquake of 1953. Thanks, however, to the individual character, the diligence and the resourcefulness of the residents, who put to proper use the assistance provided by the state, Cephalonia was reborn and evolved into a viable and modern place. The basis of the economy is still agriculture, with the olive as the main cultivation. There has also been an increase in live-stock rearing, especially of goats and lambs, with a satisfactory growth in the production of dairy and meat products. A small section of the population works in small industries, mining, commerce and, of course, shipping. Fishing has never been a particularly significant source of wealth and is limited to the needs of each household. Today, the majority of the town-dwellers work in the tourist trade. Only a few still work in agriculture. Most have adapted to the new conditions resulting from the increase of tourism.

Local cuisine: The dances and traditional celebrations of Cephalonia are something everyone should experience for yet another reason: the traditional cuisine. Some of the specialities of Cephalonian cuisine are the garlic dip, which is here made with lemon and not with vinegar as in the rest of Greece, tender courgettes, stuffed artichokes, meat stew, rabbit and the fish, which is always delicious, accompanied by a 'robola' wine, i.e. a local Cephalonia wine. Cephalonian pies - some of which are not made in the rest of Greece - are also delicious. The haddock pie, the octopus pie and the artichoke pie are flavours which one should not miss during their visit to Cephalonia.

The promenade at Fiskardo, full of pretty tourist cafes and restaurants.

Customs and Traditions

Long ago, in times quite different from the reality of today, the opportunities for entertainment were created by life itself, and especially its joys. All of life's joyful events provided an opportunity for celebration, the most splendid of which was the wedding.

The **Cephalonian wedding,** as described by the Cephalonian Angeliki Valerianou, began on the Thursday morning before the service on the Sunday. The groom's house would be prepared in anticipation, and then his whole extended family and friends would go to the house of the bride for the so-called 'handing over of the dowry'. Their arrival at the bride's house led to much running around by the 'in-laws', who wanted to provide them with the best hospitality possible. The house, decorated and festive, looked like a museum with all the items from the large dowry and the 'furnimento', the bride's gold jewellery, which on this day were all displayed on public view. Late in the afternoon, the dowry was taken to the groom's house where young girls of his family both of whose parents were alive - so that the new couple would live long - would make the bed and tidy away the dowry. Once the bed had been made they would throw a boy child over it so that the couple would have, according to the custom, many sons. In the old days, the wedding ceremony took place only on a Sunday and its most impressive feature was the large number of best men ('compare'). A 'valoutos' wedding was considered to be one with as many best men possible. After the wedding ceremony, the couple would go by horse-and-coach to the bride's house. The bride would enter the house with her right foot forward, so that the years that were to follow would be good years, and trample upon the door-mat, under which a knife had been placed, to symbolise the custom of the trampling upon of evil. The wedding was completed with a great feast, at which the newly weds would eat squabs - cooked pigeons which symbolised the purity and the goodness that were to follow - from the same plate. The custom of having many 'compare' was also common at baptisms, where there were, and still are, usually two godparents. If you meet a Cephalonian, then,

and he introduces himself with two names - Dionysios, Spyros, Andreas, Panayis and Nikos are the most usual - then don't be surprised. He just has many godparents.

There are important **religious feasts and secular fairs** at the island's monasteries. The most important of these are the splendid festivals in honour of Ayios Gerasimos, which are held twice annually, on 16 August and 20 October, and the procession of the icons of the Sissia Monastery, which takes place on the Sunday after Easter. After the service, there used to be a tremendous celebration in the area in front of the ruins of the Monastery, with food, wine, singing and - above all - teasing. The pilgrims divided themselves into groups according to the part of the island from which they came, and all day was spent in amusement. In the evening they returned to their villages, most of them far gone in drunkenness, and they would be welcomed back with shouts, whistling and more mocking. However, the teasing sometimes turned serious, with quarrels and even bloodshed, and so this custom is now dying out. Also in earlier days, the celebrations used to end with a kind of horse race, in which the competitors were mounted on four-legged steeds of all descriptions. The race ran from Sissia to Dorizata and from there to Keramies. Today, the pilgrims drive up to the

The procession of Ayios Gerasimos, patron saint of the island.

Monastery rather than walking, although they follow the procession on foot. The Monastery itself now provides neither food nor the choice wine from its fine vineyards; visitors must bring their own supplies or buy them from the vendors who crowd the site. Nor does the horse race take place any more. But the fair is still great fun and an opportunity for the locals to dance, sing, enjoy themselves and look back on the past:

> We came back from the fair in a great mood;
> we went as pilgrims and staggered back drunk.
> That's the sacred custom that we found at Sissia;
> the Panayia's icon goes by and people pay their
> devotions to her with dancing and drinking.

The tradition of the **carnival** in Cephalonia is a long and honoured one. The dancers dress in strange and striking costumes. The 'knights' wear the traditional white 'foustanelles' (kilts), tight white shirts, white gloves, tall paper helmets decorated with pretty little bells, photographs and silk ribbons. Their foustanelles are also adorned with silk ribbons and on their chests hang valuable gold ornaments, chains, watches, brooches, medals and othe'r objects. The 'dames' are young boys, as short as possible, in female garb. Everyone wears masks. Among the carnival dances, the quadrille, the lancers and the polka have survived together with Greek folk dances. The 'babaoulia', comic sketches performed by fantastically-dressed youths, are both funny and picturesque.

One of the customs which has survived down the years unchanged is that of the **'Koulouma'**. This is a holiday where everyone gets together, with much dancing, teasing, feasting, drinking and song. Here, too, the popular cantors are the most striking note, giving the feast a colour of its own with their happy songs and comic dress. They are followed by people in masks, usually men disguised as women, in rich clothes which they have borrowed; to the accompaniment of the band, they dance the quadrille, the lancers, the may-pole, waltzes and polkas, sweeping all those present into the dance. The Cephalonian 'ballos', however, with its figures and graceful moves, is the dance which shows off the talents of the locals to best advantage.

In **Holy Week,** children and young people try to

Procession of Panayia Sissia from the castle of Ayios Georgios.

*Cephalonian women in traditional costume
on a national holiday.*

scorch the long hair of ladies and girls with their candles, or to pin down their skirts to that when they try to rise it is difficult for them to do so. At the time of the Resurrection, the custom used to be for the fire-crackers to create a truly warlike atmosphere in which not even the bishop's beard was an object of respect.

Another opportunity for a good time is provided by **May Day**, a festival honoured long before the bloody events in Chicago which made 1 May a workers' holiday. In the past, this was a spring festival similar to the 'Floralia' of the Venetians. The islanders went out into the country en mass, taking with them roast meat, cheese and, of course, plenty of wine to ensure that everyone would be in high spirits. Small orchestras or the town band would often take part as well.

Among the other summer festivals was that of the **candle feast,** on 24 June, to honour Ai-Yianni Lambadaris (St John), whose day is marked all over Greece by the lighting of fires. The preparation of these fires - the main feature of the custom - was initially the job of the women and girls. This custom has its roots in ancient times, and it combines the beliefs of the ancient Greeks about the primordial power of fire with the human hope that evil can be controlled. Finally, the custom of the **bougeloma** survives on New Year's Eve and dates from the Venetian period. The islanders make 'bougela', that is buckets of water, and run around the main streets of Argostoli soaking each other.

Art and Literature

Literature and Poetry

One of the features encountered by the visitor to Cephalonia, and which can be discerned even by those who do not speak Greek, is the local dialect. It is a dialect that has an influence on the words, phrases and pronunciation of the language. Local features which over the years have been subject to the influence of the west and Venice have created an idiosyncratic mixture, which is preserved unchanged mainly in the mountain areas of the island. It is said that the people of all the Ionian Islands 'sing' when they talk, referring, of course, to the undulations of the voice, a distinctive feature of the Ionian dialect.

Cephalonia has produced many men of letters, including:
- Themos Amourgis: literary writer.
- Babis Anninos (1852-1934): poet, playwright, author historian, translator and journalist. He wrote lyric and satirical poetry.
- Mikelis (Michail) Avlichos (1844-1917): poet.
- Vincent Damodos (1678-1752): philosopher.
- Spyridon Destounis (1782-1854): man of letters.
- Elias Zervos Iakovatos (1814-1894): author, poet, journalist and lawyer.
- Pavlos Kalligas (1814-1896): lawyer, economist, historical writer and novelist.
- Nikos Kavadias: poet.
- Panayiotis Kavadias (1849-1928): archaeologist and writer.
- Andreas Laskaratos (1811-1901): writer of prose and poetry. Became involved in journalism and politics. His particularly sharp criticism of the Church led to his eventual excommunication (which was only lifted shortly before his death). Publisher of the newspaper 'Lychnos'. Writer of lyrical and satirical poems. Among his works: 'Apokrisi ston aforesmo tou 1856' ('A Reply to my Excommunication of 1856') and 'Idou o anthropos' (Ecce Homo).
- Dimitris Loukatas: university professor.
- Spyros Loukatos: historian and writer.
- Spyridon Marinatos (1901-1975): archaeologist.
- Georgios Molfetas (1871-1917): satirical poet.
- Spyros Skiaderesis: literary writer.
- Elias Tsitselis (1850-1925): historian, poet and student of folklore.

Painting

The most important paintings on Cephalonia are icons. The tradition begins in the 16th and 17th centuries, when many Cretan icon-painters were forced by Turkish persecution to leave their island and make a living elsewhere in Greece. Byzantine Cretan art, enriched with Italian elements, found in the Ionian Islands space where it could freely bloom. Among the first Cretan icon-painters to come to Cephalonia were Emmanuel Lombardos (1598-1632), Theodoros Poulakis (1622-1692), Emmanuel Tzanes (1637-1694) and Elias or Leos Moschos (1649-1686), who settled permanently in Lixouri. A younger generation followed and was chiefly represented by Ioannis Moschos, Stefanos Tsangarolas and Dimitrios Foskalis. These were followed by Andreas Karantinos, Athanasios Anninos, G. Perlingis and others. Icon-painting went into decline on Cephalonia during the 19th century, primarily as a result of Jesuit propaganda.

But a new generation of painters, who had studied in the West, followed in the tracks of the

great masters, and these artists included Pitsamanos Xydias, K. Liokis, G. Avlichos and others.

The earthquakes of 1953 caused great damage to churches and old houses, and any of the famous icons on the island were destroyed, as were chancel screens of unique value and interest.

In an article entitled 'Zografika mnimeia Kefalonias' ('The Painting, Monuments of Cephalonia') published in 'Eos' magazine, issue 58-60, 1962, Yannis Petaloudis has this to say:

"Among the works to be seen today, we could mention the wall-paintings of the church of Ayios Andreas in Milapidia, works of the 17th and 18th centuries, which have not been removed from the walls of the church, and the wall-paintings from the Church of the Taxiarches (the Archangels), which have been removed. Also worthy of note are the portable icons from the iconostasis of the Taxiarches (the Archangels) and the illustrated life of Ayios Andreas. The doors of this triptych are by Anninos, in the Italianate style. There is a marvellous icon of the Dormition of the Theotokos (Virgin) dating from the early period of the Cretan School, and a Banquet of Herod. The 'Congregation

3

of the Angels' may be Tzanes' work. All these icons are deteriorating day by day, and now in the Argostoli region all there is to see is the iconostasis at Kalligata (18th-century baroque), which has been preserved thanks to the assistance provided by Mr Vergotis the shipowner, and the iconostasis at Domata (19th century) which is regarded as the finest on the island. Also to be seen are the church at Travliata, where the old chancel screen and its icons have survived. Of these icons we could mention the calendar of saints (17th century) and Our Lady of the Angels, which is the work of Ambrose of Borino. The church was rebuilt with the generous help of the shipowner Mr Mazarakis and was decorated by Pelekassis."

In more recent years, important work has been produced by the painters Vasilis Germenis, Spyros Doukatos, Diana Antonakatou (who is also a writer), Zoe Katrava, Panayis Gevrielatou and others.

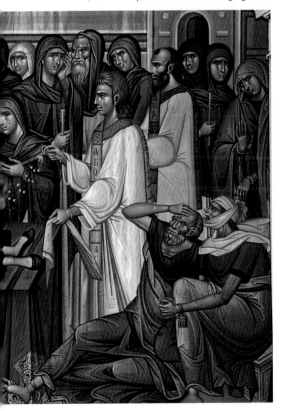

1. "The Angel" by the icon painter Angelos AD. 1600, from the private collection of G. Papastamos.
2. Wall - painting from the church of Agios Gerasimos.
3. "Initiation" ("Myisis") by Gerasimos Steris or Stamatelatos, from the private collection of Dr. Nikitas S. Kokotas.

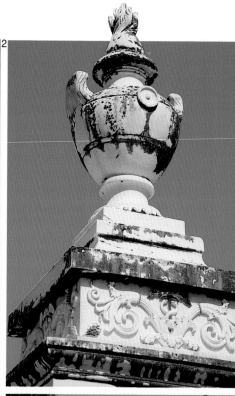

Sculpture

Alongside painting, the art of sculpture flourished in Cephalonia too. From the 16th century onward, **wood-carvers** began to appear on the island, decorating the churches, monasteries and manor houses with wooden carvings of exceptional quality. The screen, iconostasis, and bishop's throne of many churches were carved in shapes and designs of great skill and much inspiration. Some excellent examples have survived in some churches and others can be found in the collection of the Corgialenios Folk Museum.

The art of **silverware** also became important, especially from the 17th century and later. Sacred vessels, communion cups, candlesticks - all made of silver - as well as the silver imagery in relief sculpture on bishops' thrones have survived all over the island. **Marble sculpture** was also important. The marvellous work of two highly reputable sculptors of more recent times, Gerasimos Sklavos (1927-1967) from the village of Tomata on Cephalonia, and Georgios Bonanos (1863-1939) from Vouni, Pali, can today be found in both Greece and abroad.

4

3

5

1, 2, 3. Marble sculptures from the Argostoli cemetery.
4, 5. Wood-carvings from the Corgialenios Historical and Folk Museum.

Theatre

Cephalonia has an important tradition in the theatre. Theatrical performances in Greek began to be given on the island in very first years of the 19th century, and were received with great enthusiasm. Up until then, just as in all the Ionian Islands, performances had occasionally been given by various foreign (mainly Italian) groups of travelling players.

A document dated 1805 and addressed to the Senate of the Ionian Islands informs it of the wish of the governor of Zakynthos to imitate the example set by Cephalonia and create an amateur theatrical group along the lines of Cephalonia. Of course, the amateur performances given in Cephalonia were poor and ill-organised in comparison with the professional troupes from Italy. But the fact that they performed the works in Greek produced lively enthusiasm and national pride.

The great cleric and 'teacher of the nation' Neophytos Vamvas taught in Cephalonia between 1823 and 1827. In his attempts to make classical studies more attractive, he taught his students acting, in order to stage performances of ancient Greek plays on a hastily-constructed stage. The performances were given in ancient Greek.

In 1827, a rich landowner, Alexandros Solomos, turned the large salon of his house into a theatre, and this house, which stood near the church of Ayios Nikolaos Tsimaras, was for many years the focal point of the theatrical world of Argostoli.

Performances were given there by opera companies and theatre groups invited across from Italy. The foundation of a new theatre was decided upon in order to provide better conditions for the organisation and holding of theatrical performances. The theatre which was built was named 'Cephalus', after the island's mythical hero. Building was finished towards the end of 1859, and the inauguration was a matter of great pomp and splendour.

The first performance given was of Verdi's 'Traviata'. Performances began in the autumn, and lasted until the beginning of Lent each year. The theatre was used mainly for performances given by Italian opera troupes, each work being performed for 15-20 performances, an unusually large number for those days.

Cephalonian amateur companies also used the building, of course, and there were infrequent visits from amateur groups based on other islands. Interest in the theatre took a new upswing in 1867, with the foundation by a group of progressive young people of an 'Association of Friends of Drama'. The Association usually performed Italian works in translations prepared by the Lixouri painter Nikolaos Xydias.

Among the Association's most praiseworthy efforts was its attempt to seek out and put on works by local authors. In 1871, the first triumphant performances were given in the 'Cephalus' Theatre of the five-act drama in the ancient style entitled 'Enareti' by the journalist and author Elias Zervos Iakovatos. The work's success was so great that it was revived on numerous occasions until 1889.

The same year, 1871, also saw performances of two other works by local authors: the four-act tale of adventure entitled 'I paradoxos apeleftherosis' ('The Strange Liberation') by the 18 year-old Spyridon E. Rikkis and the tragedy 'Ioulianos o paravatis' (Julian the Apostate) by Theophrastos I. Typaldos.

In the following year, the theatre was packed out for the performances of the patriotic work 'I katachtonoi', a drama in four acts by Spyridon Livadas. The work was a dramatised chronicle of the frightful conditions under which life was lived during the years of British rule. Another work by Livadas, entitled 'Treis kai tessera' ('Three and Four'), a tragedy in three acts, was first presented in 1875. The title of the play was taken from the punishment by the British of the supporters of the Radical Party - three days' imprisonment and a fine of four thalers. Another work by the same author, the three-act historical play Elias Miniatis, was also a success.

In March 1876, another great success for the 'Cephalus' Theatre and its associates was scored by the only woman dramatist in the history of Cephalonia, Aspasia Elia Zervou Iakovatou, with her three-act romantic adventure 'Arsakis and Isminia', which set the whole island talking. Many original Greek works were also performed in the summer season, at the 'Apollo' outdoor municipal theatre, which was opened later. Lixouri, too, had its share of theatrical activity during the 19th century. Performances by enthusiastic amateurs were first given there in 1830. The chief inspirer of these performances was the painter Nikolaos Xydias, who translated comedies and tragedies from Italian and French. He also directed the plays, with Georgakis Dellaportas and Antzoulakis Iakovatos as his assistants.

A number of original comedies by the illiterate Lixouri poet Cosmas Canelletis Montessantos were received with particular enthusiasm. One of these, entitled 'O stratiotis gambros' (The Soldier Bridegroom), dictated by the poet to his amanuensis, was published in 1883 by the Cephalonian printing and publishing house 'Echo'.

No theatre was actually built in Lixouri in the 19th century. Amateur performances were given in the largest sitting-rooms available, or in currant warehouses, which Xydias and his associates became adept at converting into makeshift theatres. Some performances were given in the main hall of Lixouri Town Hall.

One of these has a special place in the history of the theatre in Cephalonia: the summer examination performance given in 1896 by the pupils of the local Girls' School. They performed 'Euripides' 'Iphigenia in Tauris' in a translation into modern Greek by the school's headmistress, Zenobia Halouchou, who also directed the play.

The Lixouriots were very enthusiastic about the performance, and, continuing the long tradition of dispute and competition with Argostoliots, lost no time in praising it to the detriment of the performances given in the island's capital. The inhabitants of Argostoli were enraged by this slight on their theatrical talents, and insulting remarks in the worst possible taste were exchanged.

At that point, Georgios Boukouvalas, teacher of Greek and inspector of primary schools for the island, undertook a peace initiative to calm everyone down. He translated into modern Greek the 'Medea' and the 'Hippolytus' of Euripides, and formed a company of schoolteachers and schoolmistresses to present them. Performances were given both at the 'Cephalus' Theatre in Argostoli and in the Town Hall at Lixouri.

Music

It was only to be expected that Western - and especially Italian - music would have a major effect on the Ionian Islands, since it had already reached France and Britain from the beginning of the 17th century. Nonetheless, the popular music and classical music of the islands was not just a blind imitation of Italian models. It has features and a style entirely its own.

In his article 'The Arieta and the Cantada in their true Cephalonian Style' ('Eos' magazine, issue 58-60, 1962), the Cephalonian music teacher and scholar Spyros A. Skiadaressis has this to say:

"The arieta was born In Lixouri, where it continues to be sung in the traditional way, and from there it went to Argostoli and then crossed to Zakynthos, where it was cultivated with real passion and where its name has been changed to 'arekia', perhaps derived from the Italian 'a orecchio' (by ear), i.e. a song which is interpreted according to the singers' acoustic perception. My unforgettable teacher Dionysios Lavrangas who, with his work as a composer, established the Neo-Hellenic Music School and Greek Melodrama, once told me that although there can be no doubt that Lixouri was the home of the arieta, there was no way of knowing exactly when it was first heard. It does, however, seem to have been known at the beginning of the last century. According to him, it was sung by three voices, and later by four, a form it has retained to the present. On rare occasions, we find arietas sung by five voices.

Traditional Cephalonian musicians.

"The arieta was and continues to be sung in Lixouri mainly by the 'tratoloi' - that is, by those fishermen who use nets (the trata) and who get together in the evenings in the popular tavernas in the pre-earthquake quarter known as Panagopoula. They meet after a day's toll at the nets in order to divide up amongst themselves the profits from the day's fishing. Then, sitting round the 'tavolini' (tin-topped table) or the 'mango' (a large wooden table), sipping their 'robola' (local sweet wine), accompanied by a few olives or some 'pretza' (local white cheese), depending on the state of their finances, the sharing out begins. This may start with quarrels, but will soon turn to joking, as the fishermen tease one another in their inimitable way. Then the desire to sing will come upon them. Conversation stops, and the leader of the group, who is usually the 'primos', that is the tenor, will begin to sing, by himself and towards the top range of his voice, the arieta he has chosen, which might be this one:

On the window where you lean no carnation is befitting. You are the carnation and whoever has eyes can see it.

"The other singers in the group will listen in silence, taking care to pinpoint the key in which the song is being sung. At a certain point they come in, and their harmony provides a cunningly-woven veil for the charming but naked line of the tenor's melody.

They sing together to the end of the arieta, sunk in passionate enjoyment of their music, without any instrumental accompaniment. It is this absence of guitar accompaniment which makes one admire the skill of these local singers all the more, as they manage not only to maintain the correct key, but also to keep the original tone, without sliding, to the end of the song.

"The **cantada,** which belongs to the same family as the arieta, differs from it in that the 'primos' does not begin the song by himself. The whole group sings together, and must be accompanied by a guitar, which plays an introduction to set the key and the rhythm for the rest of the group.

Of course, the guitarist is far from being a trained musician, and improvises his 'accompaniamento', which contains interesting harmonious combinations and rhythmic effects - the most impressive of which is the 'arpeggio', i.e. playing of chords in a fast tempo."

Among noted Cephalonian composers are the following:
Georgios Lambiris, Dionysios Lavrangas, Nikolaos Tzanes Metaxas,
A. Evangelatos, D. Chorafas,
A. Kounadis, G. Sklavos,
and S. Stathis.

1

1. Traditional dance at the festival of Ayios Gerasimos.
2. The 'syrtos' (swing) dance of Cephalonia.

Dance and Traditional Instruments

In an article entitled 'The Cephalonian balos' in 'Eos' magazine, issue 58-60, 1962, Dimitris S. Loukatos, university professor, writes:

"There are many Cephalonian dances, which can still be seen at festivals and carnivals. They are best danced in open spaces. Modern dancing to music played over the radio or a jazz band has dominated dance halls and summer night clubs. The old high-society dances (from polka to quadrilles) were another kind. These have become traditional in the Eptanisia and are danced either in indoor halls or even out in the countryside. Whenever there is a religious feast (panigyri) or organised community carnival (maskara), the village dances become, once again, the focal point. These dances helped develop the folk song (couplet) and music which, played by local musicians (violin, guitar), accompanied the island's dextrous dancers.

"There are many names for these dances, some of which are to be found in varied forms. Here are some: Vlacha, Voskopoules (or Mokopoules), Yires, Yirouzato (or Palio), Dilinatiko, Divaratiko, Diplo, Zonaratiko (or Zonarato), Thiniatiko, Kalamatianos (a local variety), Koutsos or Koutsos-Stamatistos (or Manetas or Mermingas), Balos, Pylarinos, Sartistos, Stavrotos, Syrtos (local variety)."

Further on in his article, Dimitris Loukatos notes that most of the songs to which the local population danced were sung 'by mouth' i.e. without any musical accompaniment. One person would start off singing the first lines of the songs, and the others followed, repeating the lyrics in exactly the same way.

The first musical instruments were the skortsabouno (a kind of bag-pipe) and the flute, which shepherds used, both of which constituted an evolution of the ancient Greek flute and bag-pipe. The ancient melodies did not have the same fate as the musical instruments. Each self-taught shepherd was so proud and sure of his own musical abilities that he considered the simple reproduction of the melodies to be an insult and felt that he was obliged only to create new ones. This fact had a negative repercussion on the continuation of tradition.

When Alexandros Solomos founded the famous 'Solomos Theatre' in 1827, he of course did not use the pipes and skortsabouno in his orchestra. Even so, the fact that already in 1827 he was able to put together an orchestra made up almost entirely of musicians from the island - the exception being the conductor, who was brought over from Italy, the most musically advanced country of the period - demonstrates that, well before the foundation of the theatre, there were hotbeds of musical talent, which the theatre later put to good use.

Architecture

Domestic Architecture

The development of folk architecture in Cephalonia is of particular interest. Here is an extract from an article by the architect Panos N. Tselepis on folk architecture in pre-earthquake Cephalonia (and more particularly the ordinary house in the villages and towns of the island):

"The houses of ordinary people in Cephalonia, although they had their origin in the needs of the farming family, ended up with an appearance and an expression which could almost be described as 'petite bourgeois'. There were both social and political reasons for this (an acquaintance with and an imitation of the lives of foreign conquerors), and also economic reasons, especially due to seamen and emigrants, who came back to the island with money, objects, habits and ideas which were new to the place. There were also intellectual reasons (here Laskaratos played a major role) and artistic reasons (given the life led by the rich bourgeois of Argostoli).

"Despite all these influences and the changes brought about by the fact that Cephalonia is an island with a particular landscape and climate, the popular style of architecture and even the building methods used are reminiscent of the houses of central Greece. Of course, the characteristic features of this style have undergone development, since the reasons for which they exist are no longer the same. Thus the 'hayati', a half open-air extension which serves both as a room and as a workroom in central Greek country areas, has become a covered balcony in Cephalonia, and reminds one of the Italian portico. Outside stairs which are made of wood in Roumeli are here stone-built, the stone being dressed and used in such a way as to lose its primitive agricultural look. The tiled roof has built eaves, as can be seen all

Traditional examples of the island's architecture: Assos (phot.1,2,3), Keramies (phot. 4), Kourkoumelata (phot.5)

4 over the island. The frontage is carefully plastered, and arches develop from a simple semi-circle into a lagged arch. "Something similar happens with the interior arrangement of the house, which is much more functional. The rooms are built for greater comfort, the various areas are more suitable for the use to which they are put, and service areas are sufficiently large for their purpose. Toilet facilities are even provided. All these things go to make for a comfortable and happy atmosphere - at least in those houses for which there is no other reason for unhappiness.

«The mentality and temperament of the Cephalonians themselves also played a part, in addition to the reasons given above, in the development of popular architecture in Cephalonia - a mentality which knows how to enrich austerity with inventiveness, as it enriches life with laughter.

«...There is yet another factor to explain the similarity between the houses of Cephalonia and those of central Greece. This large Ionian island really is a part of central Greece, in terms of geographical features, climate, light and the colours of the atmosphere, whatever individual differences may appear to exist. The austere and bold nature of Roumeli, of central Greece, was never absent from Cephalonia. For this reason, the pointless and the excessive were never able to put down roots in the popular architecture of Cephalonia. The orgiastic baroque style, which dominated the world for centuries with the political rise of Venice (with its curliques, rings, curves, lines consisting of continuous indentations and obtrusions, all filled up with leaves and blossom, and so on) was simplified in Cephalonia into its most basic and characteristic forms, with an interchange between simple curves, straight lines and circles, thus giving the austere compositions of the houses (especially those in villages) - as well as in the gateways, belltowers and chimneys - a humble but charming austerity.»

Buildings in the typical old popular style are less frequent in the towns of Cephalonia today. Indeed, it is only in the villages that any of the creations of the traditional master-builder, with the frugality and charm for which they are noted, are to be found.

Church Architecture

The island's churches - unfortunately only a few of which survived the catastrophic earthquake - are of especial interest. They are built in both the basilica order with a single aisle, and are reminiscent of the churches of mainland Greece. Internally, their roofs usually form a semi-circular shape and are called 'Ourania' ('heaven'). Most of the churches have tall, pointed belfries which pierce the sky. The flat design of most of the belfries has a western influence, and they are called 'Frankish'. There are also tower-like belfries, and these are known as 'Venetian'. Characteristic examples of such churches are the church of the Rongi at Monopolata, Lixouri (18th century), Ayia Paraskevi Tzitzitfaton at Lourdata, the church of the Evengelistria at Kastro (1570), and Ayia Marina Soullarion.

1. The Dormition of the Theotokos, Kalligata.
2. The belfry of the church of Ayios Georgios at Michata.
3,4. The churches of the Presentation of the Theotokos and of the Evangelistria, Tomata.

1. SOUTH-EASTERN ROUTE
Eikosimia - Elios - Skala - Poros

We start our tour from **Argostoli**, the island's interesting capital, with its museums and surrounding area. After this, we have divided our tour into three routes, so that you will be able to discover the island in the most effective and broadest way. All the routes start from Argostoli:

1. South-eastern route
   Eikosimia - Elios - Skala - Poros
2. Northern Route
   Ayios Gerasimos - National Park of Ainos
   Drogaratis Cave - Sami -Karavomylos - Melissani
   Ayia Evfimia - Assos - Fiskardo
3. North-western route
   Thinia - Palic peninsula - Lixouri

Don't for

2. NORTHERN ROUTE

Ayios Gerasimos - National Park of Ainos
Drogaratis Cave - Sami -Karavomylos
Melissani - Ayia Evfimia - Assos - Fiskardo

3. NORTH-WESTERN ROUTE

Thinia - the Pali peninsula - Lixouri

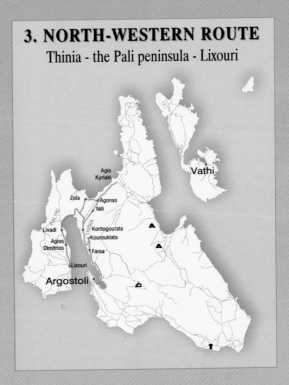

to visit

Argostoli

Argostoli has been the capital of Cephalonia since 1757. Apart from this distinction, it is one of the most attractive Greek provincial towns, with an atmosphere of its own, a well laid-out town plan, abundant trees and wide streets. Most of the residents of Argostoli, especially during the tourist season, are employed in the tourist industry. Before the catastrophic earthquake of 12 August 1953, the town had many imposing old houses, a good number of which were fine examples of the local style of exterior decoration, with elegant lines and a general aura of good taste. Among other buildings of note were the charming church belfries, built in a characteristic local style.

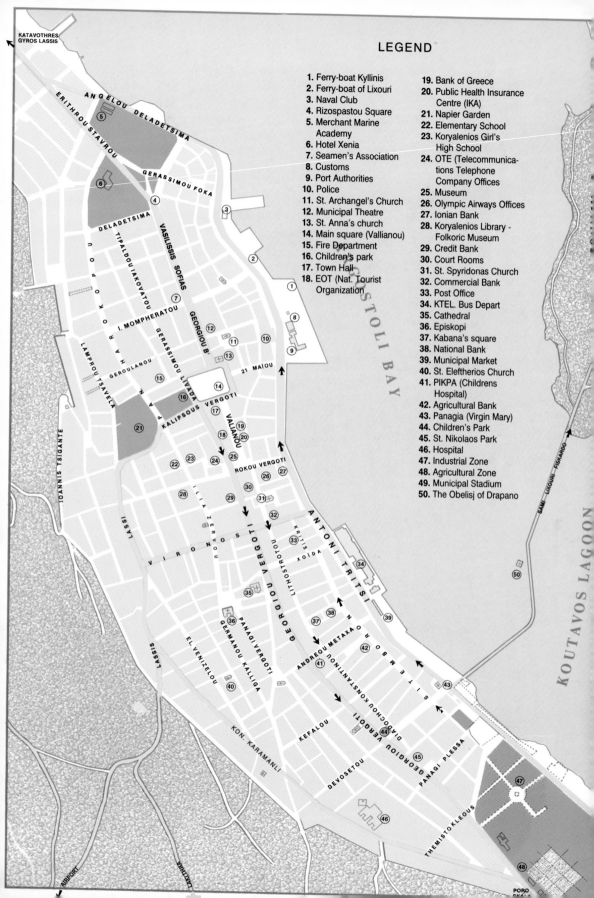

KATAVOTHRES
GYROS LASSIS

LEGEND

1. Ferry-boat Kyllinis
2. Ferry-boat of Lixouri
3. Naval Club
4. Rizospastou Square
5. Merchant Marine Academy
6. Hotel Xenia
7. Seamen's Association
8. Customs
9. Port Authorities
10. Police
11. St. Archangel's Church
12. Municipal Theatre
13. St. Anna's church
14. Main square (Vallianou)
15. Fire Department
16. Children's park
17. Town Hall
18. EOT (Nat. Tourist Organization

19. Bank of Greece
20. Public Health Insurance Centre (IKA)
21. Napier Garden
22. Elementary School
23. Koryalenios Girl's High School
24. OTE (Telecommunications Telephone Company Offices
25. Museum
26. Olympic Airways Offices
27. Ionian Bank
28. Koryalenios Library - Folkoric Museum
29. Credit Bank
30. Court Rooms
31. St. Spyridonas Church
32. Commercial Bank
33. Post Office
34. KTEL. Bus Depart
35. Cathedral
36. Episkopi
37. Kabana's square
38. National Bank
39. Municipal Market
40. St. Eleftherios Church
41. PIKPA (Childrens Hospital)
42. Agricultural Bank
43. Panagia (Virgin Mary)
44. Children's Park
45. St. Nikolaos Park
46. Hospital
47. Industrial Zone
48. Agricultural Zone
49. Municipal Stadium
50. The Obelisj of Drapano

ERITHROU STAVROU
ANGELOU DELADETSIMA
GERASSIMOU FOKA
DELADETSIMA
TIPALDOUIAKOVATOU
VASILISSIS SOFIAS
GEORGIOU B'
GERASSIMOU LIVADA
I. MOMPHERATOU
GEROULANOU
LAMPROU TSAVELA
IOANNIS TSIGANTE
LASSI
21 MAÏOU
KALIPSOUS VERGOTI
VALIANOU
ROKOU VERGOTI
VIRONOS
ILIA ZERVOU
GEORGIOU VERGOTI
LITHOSTROTOU
KRITIS
XOIDA
ANTONI TRITSI
PANAGI VERGOTI
GERMANOU KALLIGA
EL. VENIZELOU
ANDREOU METAXA
DIADOCHOU KONSTANTINOU
SITEMBORO
PANAGI PLESSA
DIADOCHOU VERGOTI
KEFALOU
DEVOSETOU
KON. KARAMANLI
THEMISTOKLEOUS
LASSIS
ARGOSTOLI BAY
KOUTAVOS LAGOON
SAMI – LIXOURI – FISKARDO
PORO EKALA
AIRPORT

These tall old buildings and towering weathered belfries are no more. But the modern town, rebuilt after the 1953 earthquake, continues the tradition of the old one in being tasteful and well-cared for, and even some of the old bell-towers are beginning to be rebuilt. Among the impressive new buildings are the Law Courts, the Archaeological Museum, the Town Hall (which dominates the main square), the Orphanage (in a wood of fir trees), the Philharmonic School, the House of the Sailor, the banks, and the recently rebuilt Cephalus municipal theatre.

The impressive Andreas Vergotis stadium is among the largest in the Greek provinces, and the open-air swimming pools are of Olympic proportions. Most of the rebuilding was carried out with the donations of local benefactors, such as the Vergotis and Lykiardopoulos families, Evangelos Basias and others.

1. *The Gentili - Kosmetatos mansion, on the old avenue of the courts.*
2. *The Municipal Theatre.*
3. *The central square of Argostoli.*

Among older buildings, the so-called Drapanos bridge, which dates from the period of the British 'protectorate', can still be seen at the harbour and links Argostoli with the opposite side of the bay. It has an interesting sequence of arches. Building was carried out in 1813, and was the responsibility of Colonel de Bosse; the date of construction was written on a plaque on the obelisk which stands in the centre of the bridge. Remains of the walls of the ancient city of Krani, with gigantic hewn stones, can be seen three kilometres to the east of Argostoli. Archaeologists date the walls back to the 7th or 6th centuries BC. Most of the churches of Argostoli are also quite important as they contain ecclesiastical utensils and icons, fine examples of Cephalonian art.

1. *Aerial view of Argostoli.*
2. *The Drapanos bridge with the characteristic obelisk.*

The Archaeological Museum

Important finds from all over the island have been collected in the Archaeological Museum in the capital of Cephalonia. There is a particularly interesting collection of late Mycenean pottery from sites all over Cephalonia. The same collection also contains bronze weapons and other small items which give a good picture of the military and domestic life of the Greeks at the period of the Trojan War. A special room in the Museum contains display cases with gold Mycenean jewellery, seals, beads, bronze swords and other items.

- Among the exhibits are:
- Fine examples of geometric and archaic pottery.
- Coins from the classical and Byzantine periods, issued by the four ancient cities of Cephalonia.
- Sculpture and pottery from the Hellenistic and Roman periods, from Sami and other areas.
- A life-size bronze head, dating from the first half of the 3rd century BC.
- Skeletons dating from the 3rd century BC from the tombs at Kokolata, at Kangelisses.

1. Head of a Roman statue, Archaeological Museum.
2. The coastal road at Argostoli.

The Corgialenios Historical and Folk Museum

The Corgialenios Historical and Folk Museum is located on the ground floor of the Corgialenios Library. It was opened in 1966 and covers a total floor space of 310 square metres. Mr Evangelos Bassias met the cost of adapting this to the requirements of a museum.

The Museum contains:

-Icons and wood-carvings from the 17th, 18th and 19th centuries.

-Etchings, maps and photographs.

-Household and agricultural utensils and tools.

-Local costumes, furniture, samplers and jewellery.

-Fine examples of local metalwork.

-A reconstruction of a 19th-century bedroom.

-A collection of old pieces of lace and embroidery.

The Local History Archive of Cephalonia

The Local History Archive of Cephalonia is housed in the basement of the extension of the Corgialenios Library. The rich collection includes important documents from the period 1531 to 1900. The collection is divided into a number of units, each corresponding to a period of history: Venetian occupation (1531-1797), the Russo-Turkish protectorate and the Ionian Republic and the British Protectorate up to 1864, and the years after the union of the Ionian Islands with Greece.

The Collection of the Bishopric of Cephalonia

The collection of the Bishopric of Cephalonia is housed in the Bishop's Residence. It contains icons, vestments and other ecclesiastical items dating from the post-Byzantine period.

The Corgialenios Library

The Corgialenios Library is a cultural institute under private law, partially supported by the Ministry of Culture. It was founded in 1924, with a bequest from Marinos Corgialenios (or Corgialenia). The building was destroyed in the 1953 earthquake, and rebuilt with contributions from various benefactors. The Library contains some 46,000 volumes, and lectures are held in its main hall. This wing of the building also contains Panayis Charokopos' collection of Byzantine icons and a small concert hall.

Views of the entrance and rooms of the Corgialenios Historical and Folk Museum.

From Argostoli we can follow several short routes to the natural beauties
and sites around the town. These are:

The tour of Lassi, which includes the 'Katavothres' (a geological
phenomenon), the British lighthouse at Ayii Thedori, and the cosmopolitan
beaches of Makri and Plati Yialos, which have been awarded the European
Union blue flag.

The tour of Koutavos with the lagoon and the ancient city of Krani.

The tour of Livathos with the small traditional villages south of
Argostoli, where the Mycenean tombs, the castle of Ayios Georgios and the
cave of the island's patron saint, Ayios Gerasimos, can be found.

The tour of Lassi

Lassi is the small peninsula north of Argostoli. It is the most touristic and developed part of the island. One route starts from the north of Argostoli. The road ascends in a north-westerly direction, alongside the sea. Close to the turning south-west, at the entrance to the pretty natural lake, there are the **Katavothres**, a typical example of the island's geological make-up. Turning along the road away from the Katavothres, in a south-westerly direction, you will return to the town, to the Faraos - or lighthouse - hill.

1, 2. Katavothres.
3. Plati Yialos at Lassi.

Of course, the tour of Lassi can also be made going in the opposite direction (starting from the Faraos hill in a north-westerly direction). In the same area is Ayios Thanasis (after which the small church is named).

Towards the bay of the peninsula you can see the pretty circular lighthouse, which was built in accordance with its oldest design. From the Faraos hill, the road descending to the left brings you to the crossing with the road popularly known as Konismataki. From Konismataki, beneath Faraos hill, following the asphalt road to the left (south-east), you will be able to take a delightful walk to two beautiful beaches - **Makri and Plati Yialos.** Further down you will be able to see the small islet of Vardiani. There are modern bathing and tourist facilities at Plati Yialos.

The tour of Koutavos

The road runs along the head of Argostoli bay, and the banks of the Koutavos lagoon.
The old bridge with its many arches separates this from the harbour. This is a pleasant drive, with the sound of water everywhere and an abundance of greenery.

About halfway along rises the hill on which stood ancient Krani, one of the four major cities of ancient times. The ruins of ancient buildings lie spread over a large area - mostly walls built from huge blocks of stone.

These walls date from the 7th or 6th centuries BC. A few remains of a Doric temple of Demeter also survive. In the Argostoli Archaeological Museum there is a plaque bearing the inscription 'Triopis (dedicates) to Demeter and her daughter - Persephone'.
The name of the woman who dedicated the plaque is indicative of the strong links between Cephalonia and Messenia, as Triopas was the father of the mythological heroine Messene.

The hill on which the ancient city stood also bears the Argostoli aqueduct, locally known as Neromana, 'the water mother', and a little further up, in a cave, is the small church of **Ayia Barbara.** Note too the pretty spot known as Myli (mills), above the bridge.

The Tour of Livathos

A delightful region of Cephalonia stretches out a little below (south-east) Plati Yialos, with pretty villages and a picturesque landscape. From Argostoli there are three roads that lead to this part of Livathos. One is that from Plati Yialos. It continues in a south-easterly direction and passes through the villages of Minies, Svoronota, Sarlata, Tomata and Kalingata. The finely-worked wooden screens in the churches of the last two villages are definitely worth a visit. The international airport of Cephalonia is located between Minies and Svoronota.

In the church of the Theotokos at the village of **Tomata** aside from the wonderful screen you will also see the hastily-constructed coffin in which the sailor G. Sklavos took the relics of Patriarch Grigorios V to Odessa. The other road (the central) going in a south-easterly direction comes out at the south-west side of the town and passes through the villages of Spilia, Helmata, Kombothekrata and Lakithra.

At **Lakithra,** the festival of Ayia Anna is held each year on 25 June, with much commotion and a lively atmosphere. Below Spilia is the cave where Ayios Gerasimos, the patron saint of the island, stayed as a hermit before he chose the valley of Omala as his permanent abode. After the earthquakes of 1953, which caused much damage on the island, a pretty small, wooden church was built in front of the cave. The location is lovely and the view astounding. To the east of Lakithra (which was rebuilt by the French) the road continues to the village of **Metaxata.** Lord Byron stayed here for four months, and it was from here that, in 1823, he headed for Messolonghi. After Metaxata is the village of Kourkoumelata.

1. The Vallianos mansion at Keramies.
2. The church of Ayia Anna at Lakithra.

Kourkoumelata is a modern village which was rebuilt with generous donations from the Vergotis family after the earthquakes of 1953. It has a good stadium, and the Cultural Centre is housed in a beautiful neo-classical building, whilst the houses are distinct for the diversity and joyfulness of their designs. The view across the Ionian Sea, to the small island of Dia and with Zakynthos in the distance, is exceptional.

Continuing along this road in a southerly direction we encounter a junction, the left-hand branch of which ends at the village of **Keramies,** where Panayis Vallianos, the great benefactor to the nation, was born. The central branch takes us to the villages of Upper Livathos, full of greenery and flowers. These are Kleismata, Spartia, Koriana and Pesada (an exceptionally beautiful sea captains' village, with many old houses).

The pretty village of **Koriana** has preserved a very ancient name. Korianna was what the Myceneans called the tasty plant coriander, as can be seen from the tablets written in the Mycenean Linear B script. Coriander -in modern Greek, couliandro or coliandro- has therefore been known in Greece for a period of over 3,500 years.

Spartia, which is situated further up from the other villages, has a long naval tradition. In the 19th century its fleet was composed of over 90 sail-boats which were used for trade, travelling to the Black Sea and as far as Gibraltar. In some of the old houses of this delightful village the visitor can see the remnants of buildings and objects that the inhabitants used to ward off pirate attacks. At Spartia was born the revolutionary Vangelis Panas, leader of the Cephalonian contingent in the War of Independence, who crushed the Turko-Albanians at the battle of Lala. At Spartia also was born the famous doctor Fotinos Panas, whose work is celebrated even today in France. The small harbour in which the Spartians moored their sail-boats is to the south of the village, at a distance of about 1,200 metres. The trip to the harbour offers the visitor the rare combination of peaceful green hills and wild gorges.

Pesada is very close to Spartia, in an easterly direction. This beautiful village was the capital of the Municipality of Upper Livathos.
The historical church of the Evangelistria, which was

built by the Inglesi family and has its feast on 25 March, is worth seeing. Further to the east, towards the coast and very near to Pesada, is the monastery of the Estravromenos (the Crucified). This was built in 1602 by the Valsamakis family, and is set in a magical location with a wonderful view. The magnificent mounds of Ainos rise to the north and north-east, whilst to the east and south-east the verdant villages of Eikosimia and their indented coastlines form a picture of tranquillity. From Pesada the road continues in a north-easterly direction, entering the village of Karavados after a beautiful route through vines, olive trees, plane-trees and gardens.

3, 4. The church of the Theotokos and the Cultural Centre at Kourkoumelata.
5. The beach at Svoronata.

5

The coastal region of **Ayios Thomas** stretches out nearby to the south, with its continuous harbours and clean waters. The imposing rock that dominates the area is known as the Yeronitsia (i.e. 'small pieces of the old'). In olden times, old people would be hanged from here so that they would not be a burden or obstacle to the living! The road that exits Karavados in a north-westerly direction a little further up meets the road that leads to the south-eastern villages of the island.

The third road that starts from Argostoli for the region of Livathos (the most easterly of the three) passes through the idyllic plain of Krania (yet another example of the preservation of an ancient name) and branches off into two roads near the sixth kilometre. The right-hand branch goes to the village of **Mazarakata.** Important Mycenean tombs have been found in the vicinity. The left-hand branch leads to the villages of Travliata and Peratata.

1. The beach at Ayios Thomas.
2, 3. External and internal views of the monastery of Ayios Andreas.

To the north of Peratata is the Venetian castle of **Ayios Georgios** which was the capital of the island from 1500 until 1757. The castle is polygonal with three ramparts. To the south of Peratata is the famous monastery of Ayios Andreas.

The sacred **monastery of Ayios Andreas** was founded in the Byzantine period. It is referred to as a monastery in the 'Report of the Latin Bishopric of Cephalinia' in 1264. It was abandoned after 1264, only to be reused again in 1587 as a convent. The earthquake of 1953 completely destroyed the monastery, aside from the church of Ayios Andreas, which was reconstructed with help from the Bishopric of Cephalonia and the Greek Army. Today it functions as an Ecclesiastical Museum.

In the first room are wall-paintings from the Holy Church of the Taxiarches, at Mylapidia. The layer of whitewash fell from the walls of the church of the Taxiarches in the earthquake of 1953, revealing these wonderful late Byzantine wall-paintings. Amongst the other exhibits are the shroud of the national martyr Grigiorios V, Patriarch of Constantinople, the stole of Ayios Nektarios and the tunic of Ayios Paisios (Father Basias). The sole of the shoe of Ayios Andreas is also preserved in the monastery. It was dedicated to the monastery by the princess-nun Romila, daughter of the Epirot noble Zotos Tsigaras. Romila took the holy orders at the monastery of Ayios Andreas in 1644. The pastoral staff and Holy Cup of the Archbishop of Cephalonia, Nikodemos V. Metaxas, an especially important figure of the 17th century, to whom is attributed the foundation of the first Greek-language printing press on Greek land, are exhibited in another case in the museum. The cloak of the Archbishop of Cephalonia, woven by the nun Theodora Kanali in the years between 1715 and 1721 is yet another important exhibit in the museum.

The castle of Ayios Georgios

1. SOUTH - EASTERN ROUTE

Eikosimia - Eleios - Skala - Poros

South-east of Argostoli, from Travliata and Peratata, the main road continues east. After the turning on the left to the castle of Ayios Georgios and another turning, to the right, for the Livathos villages (Karavados, Pesada, etc.), the road runs through the area known as **Eikosimia** to the south east.

Mt Ainos looms up on the left and, in the distance to the east, its highest peak (Megalos Soros, 1626 m.) can be seen. The road continues south east, through a fertile area with many hospitable villages. There are olive groves, vineyards, plane trees, and fruit orchards, interrupted every so often by views out to the quiet and isolated coves along the sea shore.

From the village of Mousata a minor road runs down to the fine beach of **Trapezaki**, with pine trees growing down almost to the edge of the clear water. We continue south east from Mousata, and soon come to the picturesque village of Vlachata, built in a commanding position on a hillside. The view across the Ionian Sea to Zakynthos in the north is most impressive.

From **Vlachata**, a minor road runs south-west, soon turning south-east and leading to the village of **Lourdata**, at the heart of a green and fertile valley. This coastal strip is watered from Mt Ainos, which also protects it from northerly and easterly winds. It is also known that reflection of the sun's rays from the sides of the mountain has a beneficial effect on the orchards. The ground is cultivated almost down to the edge of the sea, and provides the earliest vegetables in Cephalonia each year - not to say the tastiest. Tropical plants such as banana trees can also grow here. The beautiful long, curving sandy beach of Lourdata is very popular with Greek and foreign visitors.

From Vlachata, the main road around the island continues south - west. Soon we pass through the village of Simotata, and enter the region known as Eleios (this too is an ancient name, from the mythical hero Eleios). About two and a half kilometres from Simotata, on a beautiful site near the sea, is the famous **Sissia monastery,** built in the 13th century. According to tradition, the monastery was founded by St Francis of Assisi, and the Greek name is a corruption of 'Assisi'. Originally built by the Order of St Francis in the 13th century, the Sissia Monastery had become Orthodox by the

1

16th, dedicated to Panayia Sissia. The old monastery was completely destroyed in the earthquakes of 1953, and today a small church stands in its place. The most renowned treasure of the monastery is an icon known as Panayia of the Akathistos Hymn, with scenes from the 24 stanzas of this famous Byzantine hymn around the edge. The icon is the work of the Cretan painter Father Stefanos Tsangarolas, and dates from 1700. It is in the Byzantine-Italian style. Today it can be seen in the Corgialenios Museum. After the turning for the **Sissia Monastery,** the main road continues south-east. Soon, after the village of Plateies, it splits into two forks. The more southerly of these (to the right) enters the area known as Eleios, with its pretty villages facing out to Zakynthos. Some attribute the name Eleios to the many olives (elies) which flood the plain to the south, whilst others attribute it to the mythological hero Eleios, a son or ally of Cephalus.

The mass of Mt Ainos lying to the north provides a sharp contrast to the peaceful nature of Eleios, which is noted for its vineyards, gardens and orchards. This southern fork brings us to the village of Valeriano, from which a more minor road leads on south west, encircling the plain.

About half-way round this circuitous route is the village of **Thiramona,** to the south of which are some good beaches. In order to reach them, one must first take one of the pretty little roads through the shrubs and then plunge down a steep slope known locally as Skali in order to reach the shore.

After Thiramona, this almost circular route continues to the village of **Mavrata,** in the environs of which a Mycenean tholos tomb was discovered intact; the finds from it may be seen in the Argostoli Archaeological Museum.

1. *Trapezaki*
2. *Lourdata.*

Mavrata is also home to the Metaxas distillery, which produces all the varieties of Cephalonian wine. Like Thiramona, **Mavrata** has pretty little roads running down to wonderful deserted beaches.

Continuing in an easterly direction from Mavrata, we reach a cross-roads. The road to the north-west (completing the circuitous route) leads to Chionata. If we were to follow the cross-roads to the south of the central road, which descends in a south-easterly direction, we will reach the coastal village of **Katelio.** Here there is a good sandy beach and a wide bay affording a fine view over towards Zakynthos, Kyllini on the mainland, and the wide open spaces of the Ionian Sea. The village of Katalio and its surrounding area combine mountain, plain and sea, with flowing streams and much vegetation. Each summer, large numbers of Greek tourists and foreigners (mainly from France, Britain, and Germany) come to this part of the island.

The road continues in a south-easterly direction, through the village of Ratzakali, to end at the most south-easterly village of Cephalonia, Skala, passing through some of the most beautiful countryside. At **Ratzkali,** at Mounta bay, there are two beautiful beaches, Kaminia and Potamaki. At the first beach you will encounter some loggerhead sea turtles. Along the way, this road intersects with a minor road which turns north west and runs through Fanies and Spathi, near the beaches of Pronni ('Palaiokastro') before ending at the village of Asproyerakas. This village is now deserted as the residents moved to the coastal settlements of Skala and Poros after the earthquakes of 1953.

In the area of Fanies are the remains of a 15th-century church which preserve traces of a wall-painting showing the Burning Bush. On the slopes of the Palaiokastro hill a necropolis of the classical and early Christian eras has come to light.

The coastal village of Katelios.

Skala

Skala (or Nea Skala) is an attractive coastal village built after the 1953 earthquake at the south- eastern extremity of the island. One can get here from Argostoli (37 kilometres) or from Poros (12 kilometres). Before the earthquake, the former village stood close at hand on the slopes of a neighbouring hill. Apart from the pretty long sandy beach, the vicinity of Skala contains numerous quiet little coves. The views in the direction of Zakynthos, of the Gulf of Patra and of the coast of Akarnania are striking. Skala is surrounded by pine trees - which separate it from the beach -periwinkles, many-coloured bougainvillaea, jasmine, and their beautiful smells.

In 1956, a building of the Roman period which may have been a rich man's villa was discovered near the village. One of the rooms has a well-preserved mosaic from the 3rd century AD showing an altar and two men sacrificing a bull, a ram and a boar.

Skala and examples of the mosaics that have been found in the area.

A mosaic in another room depicts Envy being torn apart by wild beasts. These mosaics also preserve two epigrams, one of them in dactylic metre and the other in elegiac metre.

Approximately two kilometres to the north of Skala are the remains of an ancient limestone temple (perhaps to Apollo), which, according to the calculations of archaeologists, was built in the 7th century BC. A column capital of the rarest archaic type has survived from this temple. It can be seen in the Argostoli Museum today. The little church of Ayios Georgiac near the Archaic temple was built with the use of materials from the pre-classical temple.

Skala, with its fine combination of dense vegetation and seaside landscape, together with its archaeological interest, attracts many Greek and foreign tourists and holiday-makers each year.

An asphalt road leads north from Skala along the coast and, after a 13 kilometre drive through beautiful countryside, ends at the town of Poros. Near Skala, at the spot known as Sakkos, is the Sakkos cave (approximately 200 metres from the shore). This consists of two cavities linked by a narrow opening. The first of the cavities has a length of 19 metres and the second of 10 metres. This area has produced finds of Stone Age tools and it is thought that the cave may have been inhabited in the late prehistoric period.

We return to the village of Plateies, from which we started, in order to tour some of the southern parts of the island (see p. 77). The more northerly branch of the main road from the fork after the village of Plateies runs almost parallel to the southerly branch, but a little higher up, on the slopes of Mt Ainos.

Views of Skala.

We pass through the village of **Atsoupades** and soon enter Markopoulos, built on a rise with a panoramic view. This village is internationally famous for a phenomenon which is probably unique in the world and coincides with the festivities in honour of the Panayia (Our Lady). Each year, around mid-August, large numbers of small and harmless snakes appear around the church of the Panayia, bearing a small black mark like a cross on their heads. The pilgrims to the village call them 'the Panayia's snakes', and pick them up without fear. The snakes creep into the church, and wriggle up on to the large silver-clad icon of the Panayia inside. Some say this is a miracle, but others claim that the village is simply a way-station on the snakes' migratory path to warmer climates. The locals see their appearance as a sign of good luck, and remember that, as we are also assured by the Cephalonian writer and researcher Spyros Tasis Bekatoros, the snakes did not put in an appearance either during the German occupation in the Second World War or in 1953, the earthquake year. Another strange feature of the phenomenon is that the snakes appear on the Panayia's feast day (15 August) either after the service or after the festival that same day.

From Markopoulos, the main road turns north east and climbs across Mt Ainos. From the upland villages of Kremmydi and Pastra there is a fine view to the south across the Eleios and Kanteleio areas and out towards Zakynthos and the Ionian Sea.

To the north east of Pastra was the ancient city of Pronnoi. Strabo describes this city as being difficult to besiege. On the imposing triangular mound which the locals call **Palaiokastro** ('old castle') have survived the striking remains of the walls of the twin acropolis of Pronnoi, with polygonal masonry. The folk name for one part of the acropolis is 'Kastro tis Syrias' (a corruption of a name meaning 'castle of the beautiful maiden').

Approximately half-way from Atsoupades to Markopoulos, an asphalt road climbs to the north east up Mt Ainos, passing through the villages of Kolaitis and Arginia. According to one version, the snakes of the Panayia first appeared at Arginia.

Two small asphalt roads lead - one shortly after Pastra (on the way to Ayia Irini) and the other from

just after Ayia Irini (on the way to Tzanata) - to the picturesque mountain villages of Kapandriti, Xenopoulo, Andreolata and Kambitsata, on the eastern slopes of Mt Ainos. The drive through this area is very beautiful. From Pastra, the main road runs through very fine scenery in a northerly direction, and soon reaches the village of **Ayios Georgios.** At the spot known as Halkiopoulo are the ruins of the monastery of Ayios Nikolaos, in which the nuns from the nearby convent of Panayia of Atros sought refuge from the Turks in 1598.

From Ayios Georgios, a minor road leads to the north east and links the villages Kanello and Asproyerakas. From Asproyerakas a minor road leads east to the village of Anninata and from there climbs to the north west before joining the minor coast from Skala just before the large village of Poros. The exciting drive along the main road continues to the north of Ayios Georgios, along the back (eastern) side of Mt Ainos. Before long, in a verdant valley where the noise of flowing water is loud, we come to the pretty village of **Ayia Irini,** also known as Arakli (a corruption of the place-name Herakleio, linking the site with the mythical hero and demi-god Herakles). The attractive Poros

valley continues to the north and north - east, while the main road climbs out of Ayia Irini to the north.

Before long we come to the village of **Tzanata,** which also stands among dense greenery and amid flowing streams which come from the well-known lake of Avythos.

From Tzanata, a minor road leads north-west and climbs up the mountain massif in the direction of the peak known as Kokkini Rachi, which can be seen rising imposingly in the background. The road crosses the **Pyrgi** area, a place of fascinating mountain beauty. Pyrgi is known for its live-stock products and in particular for its excellent cheese. The road passes through the pretty upland villages of Ayios Nikolaos, Digaleto, Harakti and Tsakarisianos and then turns in a more northerly direction before passing through the village of Koulourata and reaching Zervata.

[The other side of Zervata can also be reached by a branch of the main Argostoli - Sami road.]

Near the road close to Ayios Nikolaos and at an altitude of 300 metres stands the famous **lake of Avythos** (also known locally as Akoli). This is a large body of water which is constantly

being renewed by springs. In effect, the lake is nothing more than a large spring with abundant water which turns water-mills and irrigates the surrounding area before running downhill and flowing into Poros Bay through an attractive narrow gap. The two names of the lake both mean 'bottomless' or 'unfathomable', and it is difficult to discern exactly where the bottom of the lake reaches. On the other side of the mountain, at the same altitude, there was a smaller lake known as Mikri ('small') Avythos. The water flow here was as powerful as that in the large spring. Scientists have claimed that the smaller lake was fed from the larger, on the principle of 'communicating vessels'. Today, the smaller lake has dried up, after works carried out to increase its supply.

In the Tsakarisianos area the minor road forks; the western branch runs for ten kilometres across Mt Ainos and joins a branch of the main Argostoli-Sami road, which climbs up towards the highest point of the mountain ('Megalos Soros'). From Tzanata, the main, road continues north east and, after four kilometres, reaches the large village of Poros.

Poros

Poros is a pretty, picturesque village that was built after the earthquake of 1953 to house the inhabitants of the surrounding mountain villages of Asproyerakas and Riza, and some from Tzanata, Anniata and Kabitsata. Its lake constitutes an excellent communications node for Cephalonia with the rest of Greece. The boundless indented coastline, 2 km. long, is full of sandy beaches and small coves. Here, you may come across the protected species of the Mediterranean monk seals and loggerhead sea turtles. Those four kilometres, through the so-called 'Poros gap' are a trip of unique interest for nature-lovers, and remind those who have travelled in central Greece of the Tempe Gorge in miniature. There is dense and varied vegetation, with imposing wooded hillsides, streams, abandoned watermills and torrents combining to form

The Poros Straits.

a scene of unique beauty. This is the most verdant part of the island. The Poros ravine is also of exceptional beauty. A steep gorge with sudden, perpendicular slopes, which is also associated with wonderful mythological tales which claim that Herakles passed through here. There are a number of awe-inspiring depressions in the rock and other marks in the plain which are said to be his gigantic footprints.

Here is the description of Poros given by the writer and scholar Tassos Zappas in his book 'Through the Ionian in a Boat', published in 1938:

"... We got to Poros about two. A good little harbour - though not when the wind comes from the east - with a few fishermen's houses. A flat, sandy, sea-bed, of the kind that calls out to you to drop anchor and swim. A picturesque place and attractive, full of vegetation..."

On the Tzanata-Poros road, about 1 kilometre before Poros, there is a small road, difficult to pass, leading to the Monastery of **Panayia Atros,** at the peak of an impressive pyramidal hill, at an altitude of 500 metres. This is the oldest Monastery on Cephalonia, being mentioned in a 'Report of the Latin Bishopric of Cephalinia' of 1264. The monastery has an impressive view in all directions, and its sunsets are especially memorable.

Views of Poros: the ravine, the port and the beach.

The Drogarati Cave

2

The Drogarati cave is one of the most spectacular caves of Greece. It is three kilometres outside of Sami and near to the main Sami-Argostoli road. It is part of the township of Chaliotata, which has been administering it as a tourist site since 1963. The name of the cave refers to a myth, according to which a dragon lived in the cave. The cave is 40 kilometres deep from the surface of the earth. Its origins have been lost in the midst of time, although the most likely version is that the cave was created by a falling section 900 years before the earthquake. To the left and right of the entrance are some large stalagmites whilst, in the depth, there is a open area of 1000 square metres, which has stunning acoustics and where concerts are given. Stalactites are the crystal formations that hang from the roof of the cave, whilst stalagmites are those which rise from the floor.

The stalactites are formed by rain water, which seeps through from the surface of the earth, permeates through the rock above the roof of the cave, dragging with it substances such as iron, copper, salt, lime, metals, etc. This results in a 'drip' formation which gradually increases in size.

1. Ainos.
2, 3, 4. Views of the Drogaritis cave.

The different colours that the stalactites and stalagmites can have is due to the variety of substances that the rain water permeates until it solidifies. Over the years, the stalactites and stalagmites merge together to form columns. The stalactites and stalagmites to be found in the Drogarati cave are over 10,000,000 years old (one centimetre is formed every 100 years) and are found beyond the concert area as well. This concert hall has a surface area of 30 x 34 metres and is 15 metres high. It can seat 1000 people for six hours without any problems being created in the oxygen supply. The temperature of the concert hall is a steady 18 degrees celsius throughout both the winter and the summer. As you wander around the cave you will encounter crystalline human figures, upturned towers, horses' legs, castles and whatever else your fantasy can discern. The impressions are unique. The stalactites and stalagmites were not disturbed even by the large earthquake which shook the island in 1953.

On the contrary, much damage was caused before the cave was properly organised as a tourist attraction in 1963 by passers-by who would descend into it with ropes and rope-ladders (carrying pieces of wood on their backs or throwing them in), thus ruining many of these natural beauties. Despite this damage, the cave still continues to maintain its unique beauty. The only thing that changes with the passage of time is the size of the crystal formations, which grow year by year.

Sami

The main road continues northwards, and soon enters Sami, an important small town, rebuilt after the earthquakes of 1953. This is one of the island's main resort areas. Sami is built in the centre of the island, and has a gulf with a perimeter of 7 miles and a depth of 12-80 fathoms. It is a perfect docking station and a natural mooring place for many ships seeking a refuge from bad weather. The gulf itself is an important biotope with many fish. Moreover, due to its high temperatures, it is a perfect refuge for loggerhead sea turtles and Mediterranean monk

seals. Sami is a modern summer resort and the door to Cephalonia.

Boats to and from Italy (Bari, Ancona, Brindisi, Venice) and the rest of Greece (Patras, Ithaki, Lefkada, Igoumenitsa, Zakynthos, Kylline) put in here. The surrounding area has much running water and is thickly wooded.

There are also fine sandy beaches, ancient sites and caves and underground lakes of great interest. The town itself has a fine and spacious harbour, a longish quay, squares, clean streets and modern housing, decorated by numerous

flower gardens. There is also a well-organised campsite.

The two hills which stand above Sami (known as Ayii Fanentes and Palaiokastro) are notable for the remains of ancient walls, built of rectangular hewn stones, each of them about 2 metres in length. The circuit of the walls has 22 entrances. This was the site of the ancient city of Sami, which put up fierce resistance to the Romans in187 BC. In the centre of the town, on the lower slopes of the Ayii Fanentes hill, have been found traces of a Roman building, called 'Rakospito' by the locals, this name apparently arising from a corruption of the word Drako-spito ('Dragon's House'). A fine mosaic and a bronze Roman head were found nearby, and are among the most outstanding exhibits in the Argostoli Archaeological Museum.

The same museum also contains some tombstones, dating from the 3rd century BC, found in 1957 at three tombs a little way outside Sami.

1. The monastery of Agrilia at the village of Dichalia.
2. The beach at Antisamos.
3, 4. Karavomylos.

Caves in the region

Angalaki: a precipitous cave surrounded by bushes and trees. The entrance is circular, with a diameter of 30 metres, and the cave itself is 49 metres deep. Passages to the south and east lead to a lake, in which the stalactites on the roof are impressively reflected. The southern passage has a length of 120 m. and the lake is 30 m. long. The eastern passage is made up of a lake 30 m. in length.

Ayii Theodori: a precipitous cave with an opening of 22 x 12 metres. The cave itself measures 76 x 78 metres, and is 55 metres deep at its deepest point. At the end is a lake measuring 28 x 13 metres.

Ayia Eleousa: the precipice here has an opening measuring 23 x 20 metres, and is surrounded by thick greenery. It drops vertically for some 65 metres.

Zervati: a precipitous cave with dimensions of 75 x 30 metres and a depth of 18 metres. The cave contains lakes with fresh water.

Chiridoni: (near Sami) a precipitous cave with a length of 100 metres long, a maximum depth of 40 metres, and a downhill passage leading to a depression and passages containing water.

3

A minor road leads north-east from Sami to the village of Dichalia and the monastery of **Panayia Agrilia,** which stands in attractive surroundings. After the monastery, the road climbs up to **Antisamos.**

On the approach to Sami, the main road turns west, and then north. At the point of this second turn, there is a minor road to the south-west, leading to the village of Poulata.

The road continues north, soon passing through **Karavomylos,** yet another village rebuilt after the 1953 earthquakes. At the edge of the village, among bushes and groves of trees, is a small, almost circular, lake with fresh water, which bubbles up from the lake bed and runs out into the bay of Sami nearby. There is a restaurant by the lake.

Close by, near both the road and the village of Nea Vlachata, is the impressive Melissani cave, with its peculiar and charming lake, which changes colour according to the time of day. Here, too, tourist development has taken place, and a tunnel has been opened so that visitors can enter.

4

The Melissani Cave

Just two kilometres outside of Sami, near the magical village of Karavomylos, is the precipitous Melissani cave. It is partly submerged, thus forming a lake.

An archaeological excavation on the little hill to the right of the lake brought to light a clay figurine of Pan, a disk bearing a representation of Pan surrounded by dancing nymphs, and an impressive statue of a young woman, perhaps that of the nymph Melissanthe.

The main chamber is over 150 metres long, around 25 metres wide with a depth of 36 metres. The roof of the southern section has collapsed, leaving an opening of 50 metres with a width of 30 metres. The rays of the midday sun beam through here, creating unique combinations of colour. At the centre of the lake, where the covered section begins, there is a small island 30 metres long, which was most probably formed by the collapse of rocks or stalactites from the roof.

There are two hillocks on the surface of the island, with a height of 8 and 9 metres respectively. A narrow waterway between the island and the inner sides of the lake leads to the rest of the submerged lake, which is covered. Stalactites, wild pigeons, even wild vegetation at some points, bats and stony anthropomorphic figures make their presence felt both day and night, creating a sense of mystery in a cave that mythology has associated with the divine.

Mythology is always interpreted by each person in their own way, and the mythology of this cave is no exception.

The locals believe that a shepherdess fell in the lake whilst searching for her lost sheep, and the lake was thus named after her. Another version says that the lake owes its name to the nymph Melissanthe who took her own life because her love for Pan was unrequited.

It is also possible that the lake may take its name from the bee-hives (melissia) which were found in the area since the most ancient times and have been connected with souls, birth, life and death.

It is certain that the cave had a ritual character in antiquity. What is impressive is if centuries ago, before the artificial tunnel that provides access to the interior of the cave was opened, worshippers would enter the cave at risk to their own lives.

Today, small boats transport the visitor over the quiet waters of the lake, thus reducing the danger which the whole exercise used to entail but not, however, the mystery that it continues to exude.

This journey stirs contradictory feelings. The serenity of the waters of the lake counters the fear and the awe that arise as the boat approaches some dark point. Awe in the face of nature, the divine, life itself.

«Moreover, at the heart of the lake there is a broad-leafed olive tree and near this a beautiful dark cave, sacred to the Nymphs that are called Naiades. Inside the cave there are stone craters and vessels. Bees nest here as well».

Odyssey 13, lines 102-106.

Ayia Evfimia

The main road continues in a north-westerly direction, beside the sea. To the left (west) rises the main mass of Mt Ayia Dinati (highest peak 1,131 m). The water on our right (to the east) now forms part of the bay of Ayia Evfimia, a pretty little town with a picturesque harbour. It lies 10 kilometres from Sami. The town is well-planned with wide streets, and there is plenty of greenery. Its harbour is used just by private boats and is the only harbour on the island which has currents and water that is no longer used by ferry services. We have now entered the northern part of Cephalonia, known as Pylaros, with its many attractive mountain villages.

Pylaros belongs to the Municipality of Pylarion. The region is bounded by the sea at Ayia Evfimia and Myrto and the mountains of Ayia Dynati to the south and south-east and Kalon Oros to the north and north-east. A characteristic feature of the region is the excellent quality of its agricultural products. The feta cheese of Pylaros, its meats, thyme honey and traditional bread are just a few examples.

The main road leads north-west from Ayia Evfimia, crossing the small plain between Mts Ayia Dinati and Kalonoros, the highest peak of which reaches 901 metres. About a kilometre from the little town of Ayia Evfimia the main road comes to a small side road, which leads south-west to the villages of **Drakopoulata** and **Makriotika**, and forks off to the monastery of Panayia Thematon.

The Monastery stands on a hill, in a forest of holly trees, at a height of 500 metres. There is a wonderful view out over the Gulf of Patra and towards Ithaki. On the road towards the Themata a dirt road starts on our left which leads to yet another traditional settlement where the lay-out and traditional masonry constitute a unique example of nineteenth-century architecture (Tarkasata).

The main road continues north-west. Just before and just after the village of Potamianata two minor roads link up the main road with the village of Makriotika. Further to the north-west, some two kilometres away, at the spot known as Siniori, there is a cross-roads.

A branch road leads off to the right (north-east), across the most northerly part of the island, the Erissos area. Another road starts off from the same point, but in the opposite direction (to the north-west), passes through the villages of Drakata and Loukata and crosses the western slopes of Mts Ayia Dinati and Evmorfia (peak at 1,043 metres), before ending at the village of Dilinata, in central Cephalonia.

The branch we referred to above enters the village of Divarata almost at once. A minor road to the south-east provides a link with a number of other pretty villages in the Pylaros area: Lekatsata, Karoussata, Antipata, Ferentinata, Dendrinata and Xeropotamos, all of them built on the southern slopes of Mt Kalonoros in fine situations.

A minor road to Ayia Evfimia sets off just before Xeropotamos. After Xeropotamos, our minor road continues east, soon turning north and north-west and entering the **Erisos** area. We pass through the villages of Neochori, Komitata and Karia. Just before Karia a poor road to the west leads to the village of Patrikata and it comes out on the road leading from Siniori.

At the Siniori fork there is an asphalt road that leads to **Myrto** (see page 106) and crosses the western side of Erisos. This beach is a beloved subject of photographers from all over the world, and quite justly so. It is yet another example of the amazing alternation of colours and the commanding presence of the mountain massifs leave the visitor riveted. It is run by the Municipal Enterprise of the Municipality of Pylaros and has organised facilities.

A little to the north of Karia the road passes through the village of Defaranata, and then comes to the village of **Vari**. Quite a number of villages in the Erisos area were not destroyed in the 1953 earthquakes, and thus the visitor has an opportunity to admire the kind of popular architecture which was a feature of the island before the disaster.

A cross-domed late Byzantine church has survived at Vari, with interesting wall-paintings in the folk style, showing scenes from Dante's 'Inferno', or perhaps just reminding us of this work.

To the north of Vari, we pass through the villages of Plagia and Messovounia (built between hills of equal height) and, at the level of the village of Vasilikiades, we join up with the branch of the main road from Siniori. This branch climbs after leaving Siniori, leading north across the western side of the Erisos peninsula, soon bringing us to the village of Anomeria.

After approximately seven kilometres we come to a large asphalt road to the left (west) which offers us a fascinating trip in a north-westerly direction through wonderful scenery before ending at one of the island's most attractive tourist resorts: Assos.

The beach and bay at Ayia Evfimia.

Assos

Assos stands on the neck of a small peninsula. It was the capital of the northern part of the island for a number of years beginning in 1593, and was the seat of the second Venetian commander of the island.

During the last decade of the 16th century, the Venetians built a strong fortress on the small peninsula in order to protect the inhabitants from the depredations of pirates. The ruins of this may still be seen today. We enter by an arched gate. Ruins of the walls may be seen, along with the Venetian official's residence, the barracks and the Church of St Mark. The view from the fort is fantastic: Erisos' western coast, its mountain ridge, Myrtos Bay and the open Ionian Sea create images of great beauty.

Assos is one of the most fascinating parts of the island. The fort, situated on a secluded, rather high, spot was used years ago - with some modifications - as a prison farm. From up there the view all around is magnificent, especially around sunset, when it takes on another dimension from the colours of the setting sun. The peculiarity of the narrow neck at the foot of the Assos

peninsula adds to the beauty of the landscape. On one side the mountains rise almost in a circular fashion, creating the impression of a small bay.

On the other side, to the west and south-west, the water spreads out towards the horizon and the eye travels across the wide surface of the Ionian Sea. If one climbs down the rocky coast, or continues walking on the peninsula's rocky mass, one will be astonished by the breathtaking Cephalonian landscapes.

The main road continues to the north. Another smaller road, branching off to the east, leads to the villages Defaranata, Kokalata and Kothrias. This road rejoins the main route a little further on, and we continue north east.

After the village of Vasilikiades (and the turning we have already noted for Mesovounia) we pass through the village of Konidarata. Here a minor road to the left (west) links up with the villages on the north-west coast: Markoulata, Touliata, Vigli, Chalikeri. The road ends at the village of Manganos, which the main road also reaches, after passing through Ventourata.

From Manganos, another minor road leads south west to the villages of Agrilia and Tzamarelata. Shortly before Katsarata, a branch of the main road to the right leads to the villages of Mazoukata, Tselentata and Evreti, near the north-east coast of Erisos. The main road runs north after Manganos.

After about 3 kilometres we enter the village of Antipata. Then we travel east, through the village of Yermenata, and finally reach Fiskardo.

Assos, one of the most delightful parts of the island.

Fiskardo

The road to Fiskardo is a scenic one, with woods mainly of cypress trees set off by small and deserted bays.

Fiskardo is a small town which contains the most northerly harbour of Cephalonia. The name of the town is a corruption of the name Robert Guiscard, the famous Norman leader and invader who is referred to in our historical introduction. He died at sea off the town which bears his name during his last raid in the East, in 1085.

Fiskardo is the only town that was not destroyed by the earthquake of 1953 and thus features characteristics examples of the island's architecture.

Among places to visit and things to see in Fiskardo are the remains of a Byzantine church, a stone sarcophagus, a frieze showing the Dioscuri, and a depression in the rock, measuring 2.3 metres in width by 2.4 metres in depth, which the locals call 'the throne of Queen Fiscarda'.

The 19th -century traveller H. Muller was particularly appreciative of the area. He wrote that the Fiskardo region is one of the most fascinating and interesting places on earth.

A minor road leads south out of Fiskardo to the village of Tselentata.

Important paleolithic finds have been recently unearthed near Fiskardo by Professor George Kavadias of the University of Athens. In his book *Paleolithiki Kefalonia* he says of the site:

"On the northern tip of Cephalonia two small peninsulas facing the island of Ithaki form Fiskardo Bay. The village is built in its cove, and on the smaller, southern peninsula.
The other peninsula to the north has on its edge the remnants of a sixth-century basilica and the Lighthouse. It is named Fournia. Its ground is formed of limestone and clay soil, where mastic, cypress and pine trees grow - but also where small quantities of garden vegetables are cultivated among rocks and stone walls. Its ridge is not in the centre, but rather toward the bay. Out of the two slopes formed, the southern one closer to Fiskardo is oblong and rather steep.
The northern slope, facing Lefkas, is large and wide and descends straight to the sea".

"...The ground surface on the southern slope and specifically within the parallelogram formed by connecting with imaginary lines the ridge top with

the Lighthouse, the Lighthouse with the cove (to the south), the coastline up to that point which corresponds in a parallel fashion with the ridge top, and, finally, that point with the ridge top, is strewn with ancient stone tools.
Also between the stone of the walls which form the fences there are a number of stone implements, some of them quite large. The villagers use them as building material, just like any other stones".

"...On the northern slope, which is called Emplisi and faces Lefkada, there are also many tools to be found. These are mainly found near the sea, where the erosion and disintegration of the terrain have brought down great masses of earth. Furthermore, one can see many smaller implements and stone chips stuck in the ground whenever there is a collapse of the seaside rock embankment, or whenever a trail or path has been opened up".

3. NORTH-WESTERN ROUTE

Thinia - The Palic Peninsula - Lixouri

A main road leads north from the northern end of the harbour bridge in Argostoli. We follow the fine coastline of the western part of the island's central spine. This area is known as **Thinia**; it is rich in vegetation, well-watered and full of interesting scenery.The famous Thiniatiko red wine comes from the vineyards of the area.

The main road passes through a number of attractive villages: Farsa, Kourouklata, and Kontogourata, Riza and Kardakata further to the north. At Kardakata there is a cross-roads. One branch of the main road turns right (north-east) and continues through the Thinia area, among fine scenery. We soon come to the villages of Petrikata and Nifi.

About two and a half kilometres to the north of Nifi a minor road to the west leads south-west and, after one kilometre, enters the village of **Angonas.**

The road continues even further to the north-east after the turning for Angonas, passing close to the north-eastern shores of the Bay of **Ayia Kyriaki (**with a fine view over Myrtos Bay (see page:97), the larger gulf of which Ayia Kyriaki Bay is part) and runs up to the Siniori turning which we have already referred to.

Two kilometres to the north of Angonas, a minor road runs down to Ayia Kyriaki Bay, where there is a good long beach and the fish are plentiful. The spot is popular with Greek and foreign tourists, who are happy to swim in such a charming place. The pretty village of Zola lies on the west of Ayia Kyriaki bay, near Angona. The **Palic peninsula** forms the whole of the western side of Cephalonia.

The main road from Argostoli through the Thinia area reaches a cross-roads near Kardakata, at which a road turns west. This is the branch which takes us to the 'Paliki' peninsula. In this area, the ancient city of Pali (after which the peninsula was named) flourished in the classical period. Historians and archaeologists consider it likely that it was a colony of the Corinthians. It is certain that it was a stop-over for Corinthian ships sailing to and from the Sicilian colonies.

The Palic Peninsula is connected with the Mycenean period, as well as with the mythic adventures of the Trojan campaign and the Homeric tales. Prehistoric artefacts have been discovered in the wider region.

Two kilometres from the Kardakata cross-roads we come to a junction with a turning to north which ends at the village of Zola.

The bay of Ayia Kyriaki and the beach at Myrtos.

The main road bends and continues in a south-westerly direction, along the north-west shore of the Gulf of Livadi. To the north - east of the Gulf of Livadi, a minor road turns off the main road, leading to the pretty mountain village of Atheras, the peninsula's most northerly village, and to the coastal village of Ayios Spiridon, which has a fine sandy bay and is what might be called the 'port' of Atheras.

Further to the south, the main road enters the village of Livadi. We descend in a southerly direction, soon coming to a poor minor road which turns north west and ends on another minor road near the village of Schineas or Schinias. Shortly afterwards, a   minor road leads to the nearby village of Kouvalata. The main road soon passes through the village of Ayios Dimitrios and then turns south, where a minor road to the left leads to the Kechrionos monastery, set in attractive surroundings. At the nearby spot known as Mersias is Ritsata, with the estate and the house of the poet Andreas Laskaratos.

After the **Kechrionos monastery,** the road continues to the north-west, passing through the attractive village of Delaportata and ending at Schineas (or Schinias). The main road ends further south, at Lixouri.

The statue of the poet Andreas Laskaratos,
with a view over Lixouri

Lixouri

Lixouri can be reached by ferry from Argostoli, and the delightful trip takes approximately 25 minutes.

Lixouri is the capital of the Palic Peninsula, and the second largest town on the island. Its name, in the older form Lixourion, first appears in a protest brought before the Venetian Senate in 1534. The ancient city of Pali, which took its name from Paleas or Peleas, one of the four sons of the mythical Cephalus, was near the present site to the north, on the spot known today as Palaiokastro.

Two catastrophic earthquakes, one on 23 January 1867 and the other on 12 August 1953, destroyed most of the buildings in Lixouri. Now there are no old and traditional buildings, but the town is developing along the lines of modern town planning. It lies in a fertile plain, which produces mainly currants, olive oil and peas.

Lixouri is an attractive town, with wide, clean streets, charming little squares, and an abundance of gardens with flowers and trees. A dry river bed runs through the centre of the town. Small bridges connect the two parts of the town.

Many old churches with impressive belfries and rich interior decoration were destroyed by the earthquakes, but rood-screens and icons saved from the ruins may be admired in the modern churches of Ayios Nikolaos of Strangers, Ayios Nikolaos of the Miniates, the Holy Trinity, Ayios Charalambis, the Pantocrator, the Panayia of the Periingades and Ayios Gerasimos.

A number of great public benefactors were responsible for reconstructing public buildings, schools and other foundations after the earthquakes. Among these were Panayis Vallianos (who gave Lixouri the Technical School which bears his name), Dr Stamos Petritsis, who rebuilt the school named after him and the 'Damodos' Petritseio Municipal Library, Thanos and Evangelos Basias, who rebuilt numerous churches, and Panayis and Antonia Manzavinatos, who built the hospital which bears their name.

On the sea-front stands a statue of the satirical poet and intellectual Andreas Laskaratos, who was born In Lixouri. Among other statues of famous Lixouriots are those of Elias Miniatis and Stamos Petritsis, and there are also busts of the radicals Georgios Typaldos Iakovatos, Stamatelos Pylarinos and Ioannis Typaldos Kapeletos Dotoratos. Vincent Damodos, Julius Typaldos and Mikelis Avlichos are among other natives of the town known throughout Greece.

Lixouri has also produced two saints: the Blessed Anthimos Kourouklis and the priest Panayis Basias (whose bones are kept in the Church of Ayios Spyridon).

The Philharmonic School of Pali has the second-oldest philharmonic orchestra in Greece, being preceded only by the orchestra of Corfu.

1. *The river outside of Lixouri.*
2. *Picturesque view of Lixouri.*

1

Professor Dimitris Loukatos, Professor of Folk Art and Tradition at the Universities of Ioannina and Crete, who was born in Cephalonia, writes in his book 'Christmas and Festive Customs' about «the songs and 'praises' of some old-time singers and rhyme-makers sung as carols on New Year's Eve.»

"The sweet harmony of those songs and 'praises' as they are sung by groups of adults accompanied by musical instruments, especially in Argostoli and Lixouri, is one of the most unforgettable of sounds. I dare say that their proper rendition has evolved into a local symphonic music, very characteristic of Cephalonia. And one enjoys it most when one hears it fill the streets from the time the lights go on for the Eve to the early morning of New Year's Day..."

Tsitselis, who also described this festivity in an article published in 1910 in the 'Diary of Zizianos' (Argostoli), writes:

"We older folk recall the old-time special singers and rhyme-makers who would carol throughout the night about our Ayio-Vassilis (the equivalent of Santa Claus), with many rhymes praising the members of the household and wishing them the fulfilment of their hopes, ending with the request for a gift (bonama, i.e. buona mano) either in the form of money, 'rosoli' (liquor), sweets or singing birds."

2

Of particular interest are the Municipal Library and **Museum of the Iakovatos brothers,** which is housed in the old mansion of one of the most famous families on the island. The house (which survived the earthquakes and has been restored) stands on the western edge of the town, and has 14 rooms with rich ornamentation.

The descendants of the Iakovatos brothers donated, aside from the house, a library of 7,000 books, the oldest of which is a 1595 edition of the collected works of Hippocrates, a collection of about a thousand pamphlets and broadsheets and the entire file of the family's historical records.

The building also houses an important collection of art works. There are 36 fine icons, of which we might mention the portable icons of 'The Congregation of the Archangels', a work by the monk Filotheos Skoufos, and the 'Honae Miracle' by Michael Damaskinos. There are also three manuscript Gospels, dating from the 10th, 14th and 15th centuries, vestments and pectoral crosses which belonged to Bishop Constantine Typaldos Iakovatos of Stavroupolis, Director of the Halke Theological School, and many other items. The library also contains some 5,000 volumes which belonged to Amilkas Alivizatos, Professor of Theology at Athens University and member of the Athens Academy. Together with other gifts and purchases, the total number of books in the library amounts to some 20,000 volumes.

1. The Iakovatos Library.
2. View of Lixouri by night.
3. The monastery of Panayia Kipourion.

Around Lixouri

To the south of Lixouri are the villages of Michalitsata and Lepeda, attractive tourist resorts with good clean sandy beaches and emerald-coloured water. At Lepeda is the old monastery where the thinker Anthimos Kourouklis - recently canonised by the Orthodox Church - was a monk. In the northern outskirts of Lixouri, remains have survived of the ancient city of Pali, which was most probably a colony of ancient Corinth. Pali flourished during the ancient classical period. Its coins show the head of Persephone with a garland of wheat, the hero and king Cephalus and Pegasus. The hill on which the ruins of Pali stand is today called Douri or Palaiokastro. A main road leaves Lixouri in a north-westerly direction. Before long, there is another road to the left (west), which leads south-west to the pretty villages of Kaminarata, Favarata and Havdata. Kaminarata is internationally known for its folk dancing team, which has won major prizes in Greece and abroad. The church of the Holy Apostles at Havdata contains a very delicately carved wooden screen and post-Byzantine icons. To the east of Havdata, at a distance of about two kilometres, is the convent of Ayios Koronatos, set in beautiful surroundings. The convent is a retreat for nuns. From Havdata, the road turns south. Before long, it comes to a poor minor road which crosses the western part of the Palic peninsula (and the whole of Cephalonia) before ending at the old monasteries of Ayia Paraskevi Tafion (or 'Tafios' or 'Tafioi', a name which can be traced back to the Teleboans or Taphioi of Mycenean times) and of **Panayia Theotokos 'Kipourion'** or 'Kyparaion'. There is an excellent view over the Ionian Sea. Near the monastery is a cave known as Drakospilia ('dragon's cave'). After the turning for the two monasteries, the road continues to the south and enters Havriata, a pretty village situated on a hill; it has a panoramic view over the flat southern part of the Palic peninsula and the sea. This was the birthplace of the educator Vikentios Damodos. The church of the Panayia at Havriata has good

3

1

icons and an interesting wooden screen. To the west of the village, the **Yerogombos** international lighthouse can be seen flashing in the evenings.

A ten-minute car drive will take the visitor to the lighthouse, which is magnificently situated. At Plati Boros, near Havriata, is the villa of Ilias Tsitselis, author of the monumental work 'Cephallonian Miscellany', and the writer's valuable archive has been preserved in excellent condition. The surrounding countryside is of unique beauty. The nearby sandy beach of Potami is clean and has good water. A minor road from Havriata continues in a south-westerly direction. It passes through the village of Vouni and soon enters Mantzavinata. There are good wall-paintings in the church here.

From Mantzavinata, a minor road leads south-west towards the southernmost extremity of the Palic peninsula, Akrotiri, where the 'Kounopetra' ('moving rock') is to be found (this is another of the island's geological phenomena). Apart from the interest of the rock itself, the area is also notable for its unforgettable views.

Off the coast to the south east is the islet of Vardiani.

A road leads south from Mantzavinata to the idyllic **beach at Xi,** at a distance of approximately three kilometres. The beach is covered with fine reddish sand, and stretches in an arc for some three kilometres.

1. The Yerogombos lighthouse.
2. The beach at Xi.
3. The magical coast at Petanos.

2

The main road from Mantzavinata leads to the north-east through the village of Soulari to Lixouri, where it ends. This is the 'Katoi' or 'low' road, in local parlance, by way of contrast with the northern roads across the 'Anoi' or 'high' area.
The church of Ayia Marina at Soulari contains interesting icons by the painters T. Poulakis and I. Moschos.
South of Soulari there is a small bay with pleasant sand and clean sea, visited by many Greek and foreign tourists. It bears the Venetian name of Mia Lako.
After the turning for Favata and Havdata, the main road continues to the villages of Monopolata, Kalata, Ayia Thekli, Vilatoria and Vovikes. Between Vilatoria and Vovikes is a cross-roads from which a minor road affords an opportunity to visit the excellent sandy beach of **Petani.**
The main road reaches the attractive village of Kontoyenada, built in a natural amphitheatre. The churches of the village contain important post-Byzantine icons, and Mycenean tombs have been found in the surrounding area.

ITHAKI

The island of Odysseus

As you set out for Ithaka hope your road is a long one,
full of adventure, full of discovery.
Laistrygonians, Cyclops, angry Poseidon-don't be afraid of them:
you'll never find things like that on your way as long as you keep your thoughts raised high,
as long as a rare excitement stirs your spirit and your body.
Laistrygonians, Cyclops, wild Poseidon-you won't encounter them
unless you bring them along inside your soul, unless your soul sets them up in front of you.

Constantine Kavafy,
translated by Edmund Keeley & Philip Sherrard

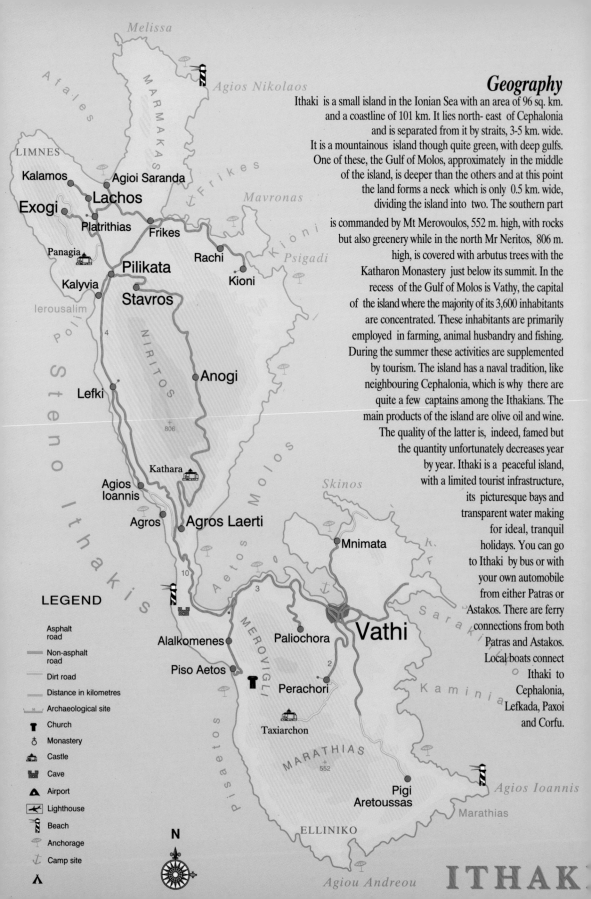

Geography

Ithaki is a small island in the Ionian Sea with an area of 96 sq. km. and a coastline of 101 km. It lies north-east of Cephalonia and is separated from it by straits, 3-5 km. wide. It is a mountainous island though quite green, with deep gulfs. One of these, the Gulf of Molos, approximately in the middle of the island, is deeper than the others and at this point the land forms a neck which is only 0.5 km. wide, dividing the island into two. The southern part is commanded by Mt Merovoulos, 552 m. high, with rocks but also greenery while in the north Mr Neritos, 806 m. high, is covered with arbutus trees with the Katharon Monastery just below its summit. In the recess of the Gulf of Molos is Vathy, the capital of the island where the majority of its 3,600 inhabitants are concentrated. These inhabitants are primarily employed in farming, animal husbandry and fishing. During the summer these activities are supplemented by tourism. The island has a naval tradition, like neighbouring Cephalonia, which is why there are quite a few captains among the Ithakians. The main products of the island are olive oil and wine. The quality of the latter is, indeed, famed but the quantity unfortunately decreases year by year. Ithaki is a peaceful island, with a limited tourist infrastructure, its picturesque bays and transparent water making for ideal, tranquil holidays. You can go to Ithaki by bus or with your own automobile from either Patras or Astakos. There are ferry connections from both Patras and Astakos. Local boats connect Ithaki to Cephalonia, Lefkada, Paxoi and Corfu.

LEGEND

- Asphalt road
- Non-asphalt road
- Dirt road
- Distance in kilometres
- Archaeological site
- Church
- Monastery
- Castle
- Cave
- Airport
- Lighthouse
- Beach
- Anchorage
- Camp site

N

ITHAK

History

Ithaki is renowned throughout the world as the island of Odysseus, Homer's hero, who after fighting for ten long years in Troy needed as many again to return to his kingdom and his wife Penelope, who was there waiting for him patiently. Thus Ithaki ('Ithaki' in Greek or 'Thaki' to the locals) became a symbol. A symbol of adventure mixed with nostalgia for the homeland, as well as a symbol of forbearance and conjugal faithfulness. As some of the archaeological finds have shown, Ithaki has been inhabited since the end of the third millennium BC. But the interest of the finds is centred on the period when the island was ruled (according to Homer) by the wily Odysseus, that is, the 12th century BC. It was then that the Greeks set off to conquer Troy and there was no way Odysseus would be missing from such a panhellenic roll-call. The war lasted for a full ten years and in the end Troy fell because of the Trojan Horse, the brainchild of Odysseus. But it required, again according to Homer, another ten years of wandering the seas for Odysseus to return to his island. It is true that Homer mixed myth with history in a very artful manner. But it is practically certain that all of his protagonists, Agamemnon, Nestor, Menelaos, Odysseus and the others, were real historical figures and the towns they set off from, Mycenae, Pylos and Sparta, unquestionably existed. The search for ancient Ithaki is still on. The great Schliemann looked for it after the triumph he experienced at the excavations of Troy. But the finds here were not impressive. Schliemann believed that the town of Odysseus lay in the area of Aetos, north-west of Vathy, where there is an ancient acropolis. Most probably the ancient town lies in the northern section of the island near the hill of Pilikata, which has produced many finds, or even in the area of the bay with the ancient name of Polis.

Several scholars question whether the Ithaki mentioned by Homer is in fact the present one. Among them is the German archaeologist Dörpfeld who maintains that the description of the great poet more clearly resembles Lefkada. But most of the details lend credence to the view that Odysseus' Ithaki is none other than the present one.

About two centuries after the period Homer was referring to, the island flourished when Corinth, which had begun to expand into the Ionian Sea, used it as a commercial station.

During the archaic, classical and the later Hellenistic periods there was considerable activity there. Two acropolises were built (the one at Aetos and the other near the village of Stavros), pottery production flourished and communications with the rest of the Greece and the east were continued.

The Venetian period began in 1499 AD. but immediately afterward the island was destroyed by pirates and then deserted. The pirates used it for about a century as a base for their raids until it was colonised by the neighbouring Cephalonians. But the soil of Ithaki is poor so many of the inhabitants turned toward the sea.

The island thus acquired a naval tradition (late 17th century). In 1797 it was occupied by the French under Napoleon and a few years later by the English. Ithaki, along with the rest of the Ionian Islands, was finally united with Greece in 1864.

*Odysseus and Penelope.
Relief from Milos,
ca. 450 BC (Louvres).*

As one travels to Ithaki, they do not hope to discover only the myths, the past, the place itself.
From Homer to Kavafy, Ithaki has become a symbol not only of a - however much desired - destination, but a symbol of life, adventure, discovery, of knowledge.
When one reaches Ithaki, they will discover the magical Vathy, the main port and capital of the island, the exquisite villages of Perachori, Kioni, Firkes, the verdant mountain slopes and the amazing beaches.

The journey will be pleasant. It will be short, almost free from any hint of adventure.
The Laistrygonians and the Cyclopses have been sleeping for a long time now.
Penelope, exhausted, will have been lost in the midst of time, whilst the wily Odysseus
lives on only in the tales of some of the island's most romantic residents.
  Divested of its mythical heroes, Ithaki might suddenly lose its grandeur too.
It may disappoint those who reach its port. Perhaps again, the island is still hiding
mythical monsters and Sirens who wait to lead astray the modern traveller.
Perhaps... Some journeys never reach their destinations.

Vathy

Vathy, built on the cove of a closed bay which resembles a port, is the capital of the island and its main port.

Its houses, which were rebuilt again in the traditional style after the catastrophic earthquake of 1953, the serene waters of the gulf in which the surrounding mountains are reflected and the small wooded islet of Lazaretto in the centre of the harbour create a picture of exquisite charm.

Amongst the features that one should definitely see in Vathy are the archaeological museum, the metropolitan church with its old wood-carved screen, the library of the cultural centre and the theatre library. The island's residents love cultural events, such as the Panhellenic theatre competition which takes place each June, the Seminars on Homeric and Odyssean Literature each September and the International Odysseus Conference which takes place every three years.

Views of Vathy in which the islet of Lazareto and the old wooden-carved screen of the Metropolitan church can be seen.

Tour of the island

Perachori, 2 kilometres south of Vathy, with 500 residents, is the second largest village of Ithaki. It is in an area full of olive trees and oaks with a lovely view of the harbour. There is a wine festival in the village every August, with many feasts and local dances. From here, a footpath leads to the ruined medieval settlement of Palaiochora, where there are churches with wall-paintings preserved. South-west of Vathy is the Monastery of the **Taxiarchoi** (Archangels) built in the 17th century. The ancient spring **Aretousa** is 5 kilometres south-east of Vathy. Near Vathy is the Cave of the **Nymphs or Marmarospilia** in which it is said that Odysseus hid the gifts of the Phaeacians upon his return from Troy. Four kilometres west of Vathy, a new branch of the road leads to the west.

Following this branch for three kilometres will bring you to **Piso Aetos,** a small harbour from which special trips are made to Ayia Evfimia on Cephalonia. Above the road is a commanding hill and the ruins of an acropolis of the ancient town of Alkomenes from the 6th century BC which the locals have dubbed 'Odysseus' Castle' and which Schliemann thought was the city of Odysseus.

From the junction of Piso Aetos, the main road heads north along a narrow neck of land to meet the beach on the right, at the **Monastery of Katharon.** This monastery was built at the end of the 17th century. It is at a height of 600 metres on Mt Neritos and is dedicated to the Panayia Katharotissa. It has exceptional views over Vathy, Aitolakarnania opposite and over the gulf of Patras.

The road from the monastery heads toward the village of **Anogi** and descends on switchbacks to Stavros. At Anogi is the church of the Dormition of the Theotokos with wonderful wall-paintings and a Venetian-style belfry.

From Stavros you will soon reach the main road, which goes along the sea with a view of the mountains of Cephalonia opposite. Below the main road is the beach of Ayios Ioannis, with beautiful sand. A little before Stavros is the village of Lefki.

The village of **Stavros** (17.5 Kilom.) from Vathy) and its surrounding area is of the most archaeological interest on the island. In the village square you will be able to see a bust of Odysseus. A little further north, on the hill of **Pilikata,** finds have proven a human presence on the island by the end of the 3rd millennium BC as well as the existence of a settlement in the middle of the 2nd millennium BC. Here, in all probability, is where the town of Odysseus was. There is a small archaeological museum in Pilikata.

South-west of Stavros is a bay with the ancient name of Polis which has a beautiful sandy beach. The cave Loizos, on its north side, is thought to have been a centre of worship for early Greek civilisation. Many clay vessels have been found, mainly Mycenean. You can go directly from Stavros to Frikes following the road to the right, or by way of the village of Platreithia.

The most isolated village on Ithaki, **Exogi,** is 5 kilometres north-west of Stavros on a hill with a splendid view.

Frikes, 21 kilometres from Vathy, is a pleasant small harbour with a hotel and tavernas. There are ferry boat connections with Fiskardo on Cephalonia and Nydri on Lefkada. The loveliest coastlines of Ithaki, with crystal-clear waters, are next to the road that goes from Frikes to Kioni (5 km.), a very picturesque settlement to the rear of a small bay sunk in greenery.

During the summer months dozens of yachts moor at **Kioni** and in the old days it was a refuge and hide-out for pirates. At the entrance of the gulf there is a partly-ruined mill. On the right-hand side of the port there are the remains of part of the house in which Georgios Karaiskakis lived after the 1821 War of Independence.

ϹΥΧΗΝ
ΟΔΥϹϹϵΙ

1, 2. Firkes. 3. Platrithia. 4. Kioni.

124

Index

How to get to Cephalonia

By Aeroplane
(The airport is 9 kilometres to the south of Argostoli)
There are flights daily from Athens to Cephalonia and from Cephalonia to Athens. There are also four flights a week to Zakynthos (information from Olympic Airways agencies; telephone Athens 9616161 and Cephalonia 41511, 28808 and 28881).

By boat
A. PATRAS - SAMI
Journey time is 3 1/2 hours, connections daily.
Patras Port Authority: tel. (061) 341002.
Port of Sami: tel. (0674) 22031.
Agency in Sami: tel. (0674) 22055, 22359 and 22456.
KTEL for Cephalonia (in Athens): tel. 5150785

B. KYLLINE - POROS
Journey time is 2 hours, connections daily.
Kylline Port Authority: tel. (0623) 92211.
Port of Poros: tel. (0674) 72460.
Agency in Kylline: tel. (0623) 92337.
Agency in Poros: tel. (0674) 72284.

Telephone Numbers
Argostoli (code: 0671)
Police 22200
Port Authority 22224
Fire Brigade 23312, 23199
Hospital 22434, 24641
Telecommunications Company (OTE) . . .22499
Post Office (ELTA) 22312
GNTO 22248
Municipality 22230, 22240

Lixouri (code: 0671)
Police 91207
Port Authority .91205
Hospital 91233, 91975
Telecommunications Company (OTE) . . .91399
Post Office (ELTA) 91206
Municipality 91208

Sami (code: 0674)
Police 22330

C. ASTAKOS - ITHAKI - SAMI
(summer months only)
Journey time is 2 1/4 hours, connections daily.
Astakos Port Authority: tel. (0646) 41052.
Agency in Astakos: tel. (0646) 41368.
Port of Sami: tel. (0674) 22031.
There are KTEL buses daily from Athens to Astakos: tel. 5129293.

D. ARGOSTOLI - LIXOURI
Daily ferry-boat connections (30 mins.)

E. *From Cephalonia one can visit Ithaki, Lefkada and Zakynthos by boat, mainly in the summer months.*

How to get to Ithaki

You can get to Ithaki by coach or with your own car from the ports of Patras or Astakos. There are ferry-boat connections from Patras and Astakos. Local boats connect Ithaki with Cephalonia, Lefkada, Paxoi and Corfu.

Port Authority .22031
Fire Brigade 23333
Health Centre .22222

Ayia Evfimia (code: 0674)
Police 61204
Municipality 61286, 61207

Municipality of Erisos (code: 0674)
Police 41460
Municipality 51633, 51181

Municipality of Eleios-Pronoi (code: 0674)
Police 72210
Municipality .72551-2

Township of Omala (code: 0671)
Municipality 86221, 86241

Ithaki (code: 0674)
Police 32205
Port Authority .32909
Fire Brigade 3199, 33499
Hospital 322222
Telecommunications Company (OTE) 32299, 32099
Municipality 32795, 32197

Bibliography

Other books, studies and articles were used in the writing of this book:

- Antipas, Panayis G., "Η μετασεισμική Κεφαλλονιά" Kefalliniakis Estias publishers, November 1957.
-Antipas Marrinos, Publication of the Federation of Cephalonian and Ithakian Societies, Athens, 1980.
- Antonokatou, D, "Η Κεφαλλονίτισσα" Eos, issues 58-60,1962.
- Chiotis, P. "Ιστορικά απομνημονεύματα Επτανήσου" ,
"Ιστορία του Ιονίου Κράτους από συστάσεως αυτού μέχρι Ενώσεως".
- Fouriotis, Angelos, "Το Παραμύθι της Χώρας των Τηλεβόων" Eos, isssues 58-60,1962.
- Georgatos, Aristomenes,"Κεφαλλονιά και Ιθάκη" Municipality of Kefallinias, 1977.
- Geroulanos, M."Το Ληξούρι"
-Idromenos, A. "Πολιτική Ιστορία της Επτανήσου"
- Inglesis, Andreas, "Αναμνήσεις" Eos, issues 58-60,1962.
- Kavvadias, Giorgos, V., "Παλαιολιθική Κεφαλλονιά", Fitraki Publications, Athens, 1961.
- Konomos, inos,"Ο Ηλίας Ζερβός".
- Kosmetatos, M.S.F., "Περίπατος στην Κεφαλλονιά", Eos, issues 58-60, 1962.
- Kosmetatos, M.S.F.,"Το εν Αργοστόλιω θέατρον Ο Κέφαλος" Eos, issues 58-60, 1962.
- Kounadi-Papadatou, Boula "Τα γλυπτά του Δράπανου στην Κεφαλλονιά" Publications Athens, 1985.
- Laskaratos, Andreas "Ήθη, έθιμα και δοξασίες της Κεφαλλονιάς" Pella Publications, Athens.
"Τα μυστήρια της Κεφαλλονιάς" Pella Publications, A, Athens.
-Liosatos, Dionysios, E. and Georgios P. Makris "Τουριστικόν λεύκωμα Κεφαλληνίας και Ιθάκης", Athens, 1951.
- Loukatos, Dimitris, S.,"Κεφαλλονίτικη λατρεία", Athens, 1946.
- Loverdos, I.K.,"Ιστορία της Κεφαλληνίας".
-"Η ψαλτική της Κεφαλλονιάς", isssues Magazine "Eos", issues 58-60,1962.
-"Ο Κεφαλλονίτικος Μπάλος", isssues Magazine "Eos", issues 58-60,1962.
- "Χριστουγεννιάτικα και των Γιορτών", Filipotti Publications, Athens, 1978
-- "Πασχαλινά και της Άνοιξης", Filipotti Publications, Athens, 1980
-"Τα Καλοκαιρινά", Filipotti Publications, Athens, 1981.
- "Τα Φθινοπωρινά", Filipotti Publications, Athens, 1982.
- Marinatos, Spyros, "Κεφαλληνία-Ιστορικός και Αρχαιολογικός Περίπατος",
Publication of the Local Tourism Committee of Cephalonia, 1962.
-Mavroyiannis, Gerasimos, "Ιστορία των Ιονίων Νήσων".
- Moschopoulos, Gerasimos, C., "Ιστορία Συνοπτική της Κεφαλληνίας", Athens, 1951.
-Parentis, Evangelos, D. "Ιστορία της Κεφαλληνίας-Κεφαλλονιά, η πολυαγαπημένη μας", Athens, 1977.
-Petaloudis, Yiannis, "Ζωγραφικά μνημεία Κεφαλληνίας", Eos, isssues 58-60, 1962.
-Petris, Tasos, "Θέατρα και παραστάσεις στην Κεφαλλονιά του 19ου αιώνα", Magazine "Ιστορία Εικονογραφημένη", May 1981.
-"Τα χρόνια της ιταλικής και γερμανικής κατοχής και της εθνικής αντίστασης στην Κεφαλλονιά και στην Ιθάκη",
Publication of the Brotherhood of Cephalonians and Ithakians in Piraeus, Athens, 1981.
-"Κεφαλληνία-Σύντομος τουριστικός οδηγός", Publication of the Local Tourism Committee of Cephalonia, 1961.
-Skiaderesis, Spyros, A.,"Αριέτα και Καντάδα στη γνήσια λαϊκή Κεφαλλονίτικη μορφή τους", Eos, isssues 58-60, 1962.
-Souris, A. "Η Κεφαλληνία και ο Αγών της Ανεξαρτησίας", Eos, isssues 58-60, 1962.
-Tzelepis, Panos, Ν.Η Αρχιτεκτονική της προσεισμικής Κεφαλλονιάς- Το λαϊκό σπίτι
στα χωριά και στις πόλεις", Eos, isssues 58-60, 1962.
-Tzouganakos, Nikolaos, D., "Το Αργοστόλι - Μελέτη για το χρονικό και την τοπωνυμία", Eos, isssues 58-60, 1962.
-Verikios, Spyros,"Ιστορία των Ηνωμένων Κρατών των Ιονίων Νήσων", 1815-1884.
- Zakythinos, Dionysios, "Θέμα Κεφαλληνίας", Eos, isssues 58-60, 1962.
-Zappas, Tassos, "Στο Ιόνιο με μια βάρκα" (1st edition: Athens, 1938, 2nd edition: Athens, 1970).
-Zervonikolakis, Nikos, "Κεφαλλονιά, το νησί με τα δύο πρόσωπα", Fantazia magazine, 2 September 1983.

Texts: GIANNIS DESYPRIS, TASSOS PETRIS, DAPHNE CHRISTOU
Text editor: DAPHNE CHRISTOU
Artistic editor: EVI DAMIRI
Photographs: M. TOUBIS S.A.

Production - Printing: M. Toubis S.A.